For Sakinah

A Muslim Woman's Reflections On Being a Bride

For Sakinah

A Muslim Woman's Reflections On Being a Bride

Coral Qadar

MOTHERSMIND PUBLICATIONS

For Sakinah

MOTHERSMIND PUBLICATIONS
Copyright © 2007 by Coral Qadar

Published in the United States of America
by Mothersmind Publications
www.mothersmind.com

Cover Design by Distinct New Africa Designs

FOURTH EDITION

ISBN 978-0-6151-5555-5

www.forsakinah.com
info@mothersmind.com

For mommy and "my women."

Acknowledgements

I must first thank, ever so much, my husband, Lateef, for challenging me to write and to become a better writer. Thanks to Muminah, Farah and Yumnah who are the very best support persons, proofreaders, editors, sounding boards, etc. any writer could possibly have. And thanks to Ismail, Bilal, Muhammed and Hanif for your love and encouragement. To Maria and Margarita, who heard me calling for help and always answered, thank you. I also realize that there are both strong and subtle influences, in several essays, from other women whose lives have influenced mine as a woman and as a wife—especially O.G., Islah Umar, Kim Bilal Rashada, Kareema Medina Bilal and so many other Muslim women I could not possibly list them. Please know that I love you all! Special thanks also, "Aunt" Delsie, Rhoda Woods, and Frances, who inspired me to "dance!" Thanks to Dr. Zakiyyah Muhammad, Natalie G. Owen and Lorraine Lamont for proofreading and Zakiyyah NuMan for proofreading and so much nourishment! Thank you, Zaimah Habeeb, Muslimah Bilal, Imani Bilal and Kauthar Umar for picking my brain about marriage. Thank you, Khareemah Shabazz and Becca Nu'mani, for graciously investing in my dreams. Thanks to Nishel Taufeeq, Sarah Woods-Shah, Ihsan Naji, and Aminah Adesanya for rescuing me on those challenging ante-partum and postpartum days. Also, to Barbara for your unyielding support and to my sister Deirdre for your love. So much immense gratitude to Anika Sabree and Distinct New Africa Designs for our lovely cover design. Shirley Hamid, you are an inspiration! Thank you to Ameenah Muhammad Mujahid, whose recent marriage inspired me to "deliver" that which I had conceived so long ago. And finally, thanks ever so much to my imam, W. Deen Mohammed. No words could come close to expressing my gratitude for your healing wisdom and your unwavering service to humanity.

With G-d's Name, The Merciful Benefactor, The Merciful Redeemer. I affirm openly that nothing deserves to be worshipped except The One G-d. I affirm openly that Muhammed is the messenger of G-d. I remind the Muslim reader to offer prayers and salutations of peace upon Muhammed as well as equal prayers upon the other Prophetic figures mentioned in this work: Abraham, Moses, Aaron, and Jesus—may the Prayers and Peace be forever upon them. I also offer the Prayers and salutations of Peace upon the Quran's stated examples of righteous women mentioned herein: Mary and Asiya. I pray also that G-d's abundant rewards be granted upon Khadijah and Fatimah, Muhammed's wife and daughter—May G-d be pleased with them—for the enormous good that they have accomplished in service to humanity.

For Sakinah

Among His signs is this, that He created for you mates from among yourselves that you may dwell in tranquility with them, and He has put love and mercy between your (hearts). Verily in this are signs for those who reflect.

The Holy Quran, Chapter 30—Rome—Verse 21

INTRODUCTION

Naturally, the first question that I expect every reader to ask is, "Who is this Sakinah? For a woman to be deemed worthy of having a book written specifically for her, she must be very special indeed!" I, for my part, am delighted to respond, "Indeed, she truly is!" My answer to this inquiry delights me immensely because I have written "For *Sakinah*" as a title of tribute to the beautiful spirit of innocence that resides within every woman. The concept of *Sakinah* is actually a reference to the Arabic word *Sukun*—rest—which captures a particular state of mind and spirit. Thus, *Sakinah* is intended as a reference to the natural and healthy state of tranquility, serenity, peace and satisfaction that G-d—Who deserves all Glory—intends for each one of us to experience and enjoy. *Sakinah* is a presence, as well as a reality, that exists within each and every one of us. This presence becomes magnified when we are successfully partnered in a wholesome marriage bond. So, if you are a G-d conscious woman, seeking peace and happiness within the precious design of matrimony that our Merciful G-d has crafted, then you—whoever you may be—are *Sakinah*.

Thus, in writing "*For Sakinah*," I am writing to every woman who desires to enjoy a state of deep satisfaction within her marital-love relationship. *Sakinah* is the innocent girl that resides within all women who believe wholly in G-d's goodness and in the potential for such goodness to reign in all things. *Sakinah* is the young bride full of hopes for enjoying a special marriage with her love. She is completely expectant of achieving the tranquil and blissful state that her soul craves to share with her husband. Moreover, *Sakinah* is not only a new bride; she is also the bride of ten or fifteen or twenty-seven years, such as myself. She is the faithful wife who is ever-striving to preserve that innocence and newness within her heart and her marriage. So, truthfully, I compiled the lessons in "*For Sakinah*" for myself as well.

In these pages, I have sought to recall and record the values and ideals that have preserved my own marriage, as well as proven tools and strategies for helping any marriage to become renewed, vital and more fulfilling. I have also written these pages to share precious gifts of experiences with my daughters and to help myself remember what I have come to understand as holding the most value in life. Thus, I have written "*For Sakinah*" so that when I am lost or not at peace, I might have a compass to redirect my focus towards what has previously given me light.

The title "*For Sakinah*" is essentially inspired by the above-quoted Quranic verse. I must say that I was overjoyed when I first read this verse because it revealed that G-d created man and woman to exist in a state of love and tranquility. I, like most women, have always craved this type of deep and close companionship with my husband. I was therefore very relieved to know that, as a woman, I was normal and not simply given to some superfluous ideals of romanticism. I could see clearly that deeply held bonds of love and affection are an important part of G-d's perfect and natural design and pattern for all human life—*Fitra*. Indeed, G-d has isolated the marital relationship between a man and a woman for describing the *Sakinah* state of tranquility that we all deeply crave as being a part of our human experience. It feels truly gratifying to know that G-d, in His infinite love and mercy, intends this *Sakinah* state of existence for you and me.

The state of *Sakinah* is also suggestive of a deeply spiritual state that has to do with illumination and insight. It has been my experience that, in order to find tranquility in life, one must arrive at a state of acceptance as to how one fits into the grand scheme of things. This is to say that those who find tranquility within their human relationships are usually at peace primarily somewhere deep within themselves. They are validated in an awareness of G-d as the origin of all reality and they are, therefore, relaxed and secure in the work of loving another. They are anointed in the light of G-d's love and, therefore, feel blessed and honored to share that love with others.

As Muslims we know that illumination is ultimately both an extension and by-product of accurate information. We also know that the truly blessed forms of spiritual education are guided by an earnest desire to heal and serve humanity. We are all educated first by the love of our parents and teachers and then by our own life-experiences. G-d further grants special degrees of illumination upon messengers and prophets so as to assist humanity along the way, as we humans evolve towards our destiny of wholeness in restoring the life of the universal soul. The highest form of spiritual illumination, in my view, is when we are liberated unto awareness of and trusting in G-d's perfect, pure love. With this, we are free to love all others, truly and sincerely.

"*For Sakinah*" attempts to share some aspects of these various forms of education; yet I must disclaim having discovered a magic pill for enjoying a completely tranquil, love-filled marriage. However, the ideas presented here will surely provide you with sound, spiritually grounded tools and reminders for transforming or anchoring your thinking in ways that bring more richness to married life. I truly believe that this effort can serve to support your preparation for marriage and for the wonderful and exciting work of bringing much more *Sakinah* into your life and all your relationships.

In my own marriage, I have experienced extremes of joy and disappointment. I have also, however, been blessed to enjoy great periods of tranquility and deep satisfaction. These periods are the jewels of my marriage. Because of this, I am also still a new bride full of expectation, trust and love—for G-d, for myself, for my family, and for the man that I love. The real challenge is when we can be in *Sakinah* even as we are experiencing the highs and lows of life and marriage. Indeed, we are true reflections of illumination when we can exist in *Sakinah* in all times and through all extremes. I believe marriage to be the perfect preparation for developing this skill. Although I have been married for what is considered a long time in the modern era, I am still challenging myself daily to embrace this *Sakinah* state of enlightenment. I am still learning, questioning, experimenting, and thankfully, growing. I still seek out and accept good advice, and am always listening for the voice of truth that is always there, sitting still within my soul, the voice that knows instinctively what is right.

This voice knows that the purest education for empowering us towards satisfying our inherent urge for peace and tranquility in life and marriage comes, of course, from The Creator. We would be wise, therefore, to discover what G-d says about whom we are really created to become and what our highest purpose is meant to be. Who better to inform us as to our strengths and weaknesses (those things that may cause us to slip away from our original spiritual home of the garden) than the Creator? I have come to know and understand that the source of all peace is in understanding oneself in relation to The Merciful One G-d.

I hope that this work will be accepted as a truly heartfelt and love-filled thank you to all of the many, many women friends and family members who have shared their advice and care with me through the years so that I might become a better wife and mother. I can never adequately express in words the deep love that I have for these marvelous, giving, and brilliant women. The sisterly love, support, and friendship of so many beautiful, generous, and wise women has embraced and caressed me throughout my marriage and life. These pages have been garnered from the myriad special conversations and reflections we have shared with one another.

You will notice that these essays are not ordered in any particular sequence. This was my way of imparting the idea that we must take each of life's lessons as G-d presents them to us, not as we think that our lessons should come. Also, some essays may not be fully captured until you have read them over again or perhaps until you have experienced a bit more of married life. Finally, I pray that this work might assist many new and seasoned brides towards inviting countless days filled with the illumination of *Sakinah* into their lives.

For Sakinah

LOVE NOTES

If marriage is to offer the greatest opportunity for us to gain and reflect a settled sense of peace, we are wise to learn as much as we can about our pre-married selves. Thus, our first love notes are about exploring our own soul-selves. They are simply aids to assist you towards your rediscovery, or being more aware, of the type of person you are becoming.

For Sakinah

BECOMING

Self-awareness is essential to purposeful living. It provides us with the best conditions for perceiving when we are well matched. Ideally, our upbringing would have provided abundant opportunities for us to explore our inner workings. A stable childhood and adolescent transition allow for creative self-exploration as we discover our world and our own inner being while being protected and guided by a safe and supportive network of parents, siblings, grandparents, extended family, and trusted family friends. However, for so many of us, the ideal experience of safe childhood development and self-exploration, guided by attentive and involved parents, was not the reality.

Today, young people are often faced with carrying inordinate amounts of stress as they try to achieve self-discovery, while also attempting to cope in a confusing and rapidly changing world. Children and youngsters are also greatly burdened by the pressures their parents are shouldering as well. Most often, both parents are working outside the home to make ends meet and, thus, are relying upon educators to provide their children with some sort of reflective guidance. Many young people are left feeling terribly confused, vulnerable, overwhelmed, and wounded if they are among those whose parents divorce. They are inevitably left feeling dangled between the two people that they love more than anything, or feeling deprived of one parent's valuable presence for reasons that they sadly cannot control. Sometimes, children are forced to step into the role of the pseudo-parent as they help their mother or father deal with the depression and shock of restructuring the family after a divorce.

In addition, young people are also terrifically distracted from the important work of self-exploration and discovery as a result of the supercharged influences of today's popular culture. They live in a world that, from the cradle, triggers their brains with light, sound and various electromagnetic vibrational impulses from television, radio, games, cell phones and computers. While we are blessed with unprecedented access to information, we are also often over-stimulated by impulses and values that do not enrich our lives. This is so to the extent that we often see underdevelopment in social skills, moral reasoning, and the ability to utilize emotional intelligence to relate better with the inner self, as well as with others.

For these reasons and many others, it is not unusual today for young people to arrive at the day of their wedding without having given much intently focused time or thought to the discovery of whom they are becoming as a sacred spirit being. While they may have made some career-choice decisions as a manifestation of the awareness that they need money to buy those things they have come to desire, they may not yet have been directed toward discovering the purpose of the unique human spiritual energy that gives meaning to life and to living. To complicate matters, we also find that we are sometimes inspired to marry in our search of some satiation for the unknown yearning for spiritual wholeness. We may nurture a sort of silent subliminal hope that our husband or wife will fill the invisible void somehow; believing that the emptiness we are feeling can be eradicated through the activities and indulgences of being in love or being married. We want to be held and cuddled, as a means of affirming that we are alive, intelligent, special, and beautiful. We want someone to touch us so that we can ascertain that we are indeed real.

Yet, sooner or later, if we are truly blessed, the noise and clamor will settle and we will return gracefully to the innocent quest for self-awareness—embracing those endeavors abandoned far too early on, as we were swallowed up by all the facades of modern living. Eventually, we all must reconnect with our sacred spirit and make conscious decisions about who we are becoming.

For Sakinah

YOUR PURPOSE

The best preparation for marriage is to strive to discover, at least in part, why G-d has created you. We know that the true purpose of life and earthly existence is only fully known to The Creator; yet, in the Quran G-d does give many messages as to the purposes for which He has created us. G-d states that He has created us specifically in order to extend His Mercy to us. We are also created so that we might become truly alive unto consciousness of our G-d. With this, G-d invites us towards the idea that we are still not yet truly alive. G-d also suggests that we are created for peace and satisfaction. Indeed, our souls crave peace more than anything else. If we are created for peace, should not marriage be designed to support this end?

BEING ALIVE

What excites you about being alive? What gifts do you possess? What mark do you want to leave within the world? How do you desire to make humanity more connected? When you are clear about these things or are at least free to claim the energy of self-fulfillment, you are more capable of knowing whom you should marry. Sharing and building dreams together is really the life-blood of any marriage. When we have no dreams or desires, we exist only marginally, as if starving, and some aspect of ourselves seems to whither. This is not about picking a career or deciding what to declare as your major. This is about how you are making use of the magnificent gifts of your human body, mind, and spirit.

PREPARATION

I am convinced that the best preparation for marriage is also to become more reconnected to, and more aware of, what G-d's pattern for successful life is. This surely must be the truest purpose of all scripture and revelation. Human beings are prone to getting lost at times, but G-d has not left us alone here without guidance. From the beginning of man's existence, G-d has been communicating His magnificent plan to us. G-d communicates through both the natural world and the psyche of the ordinary mortal human being. Staying connected with The Creator's communications is the wisest means for being prepared for marriage. You will soon also realize that your new life will require awareness of, and adeptness at, many skills which you previously didn't realize married life—and later, parenting—would require.

As a new bride, you are primarily a student learning volumes about many new things. As you and your new love both reach for your goals together, you will finally understand what all the focus on schooling and education has really been about. Unfortunately, much of what is needed to run and manage the life of the home is not dispensed in traditional school classes. To this end, you will probably begin to better understand the lessons and lives of your parents. Your own mother has likely often juggled functioning as a teacher, tutor, chef, chauffeur, psychologist, disciplinarian, accountant, librarian, secretary, gardener, shopper, housekeeper, baby incubator, arbitrator, wet nurse, jailer, vacation and party planner, nurse, lover, seamstress, laundress, hairdresser, and social worker. Further, she likely managed all of these duties while also working outside the home at a full time job!

Most of us would agree that there is a serious need for young people to receive far better preparation for marriage. Don't worry, however, if you don't feel adequately prepared. Your beautiful and sincere heart is a sure match for any challenge.

HOMEWORK
If I were to give a single preparatory assignment for strengthening marriage, an assignment that also serves as a broad spectrum healing and toning potion—one possessing the most powerful ability to heal the heart,

mind, body and soul—it would be: to sit oneself down surrounded by nature during the day or night, while thinking and reflecting upon the brilliance, perfection, beauty, and wonder of the natural world. Whether we look to the skies, or within the amazing science of our own bodies; or within the oceans, the plant world, or within the mysteries of the human mind, we are humbled and, thus, we are reconnecting with the self that is truly real.

COMPATIBILITY

How can we begin to seek a compatible husband if we are not yet aware of whom we are becoming inside? Become more aware of who you are. Strive to be conscious of what ideas and ideals are operating at the deepest levels of your truest self or soul. What are your desires, motivations, fears, hopes, dreams, and fantasies? What are your strengths? What areas would you like to improve upon? What is your disposition or personality type? What do you expect to gain, when married, towards achieving your life's purpose? What do you plan to offer to your love to assist him towards achieving his?

BEING

While we live in a society where women are expected to have clear-cut goals and career objectives, I have met women whose objectives are less focused and more diffuse. They are not driven to claim any particular profession but, rather, enjoy exploring their world and gaining new experiences. In these times, a woman of this temperament is made to feel that she is somehow lacking, or that she is not as well put together as her corporate-minded contemporaries. I am, however, of the opinion that these ladies are in possession of a very natural and healthy feminine spirit, one that is actually a highly evolved state for any woman to arrive at. Our modern culture does not ordinarily allow a woman to claim this part of herself until she has reached the age of "retirement." This liberated woman is intelligent and well educated; yet, she is open and ready to experience life on her own terms as she witnesses how G-d is continuously unveiling her world to her. It is said that she has found peace at simply "being" rather than in "doing."

She tends to be delighted at having the opportunity to help her husband achieve his life's purpose and mission. She doesn't feel diminished by simply being there to support the private life of one who is shouldering manly responsibility. She enjoys the experience of learning new things by being partnered with a man who has so much to offer. She is not threatened by fear that she is giving up her dreams because she possesses a spirit whose dreams are not defined by job titles. She has found ways of actually experiencing her dreams each and every day as she wonders at the magnificence of the sunrise or as she watches her herb garden blossom. She is a rare jewel as she is free to read and learn and interact with her world. While we are kept busy proving our worth, she instinctively knows that she was born into the universe already worthy.

YOUR UNION

Like all living forms, we human beings are instinctively "wired" to mate. This is true biologically as a means for survival; yet, we know that even when having children is not possible or desired, we seek to partner with one another. Sharing the experience of living with our mate is, it seems, as essential and strong of a passionate drive as our drive to procreate the human species. Some would say that we are compelled by a need to find mirrors for ourselves, so as to have the best part of ourselves reflected back to us as a way of affirming our own human beauty and value through the eyes of another beautiful human being. While I believe that to be true, I have come to think that marriage is a vital spiritual exercise towards preparing ourselves to become liberated as we are reunited with the universal soul. I believe that marriage has something to do with preparing us for eternal life as we learn to accept the wholeness of others. We see in our husbands and children new reflections of the human essence. We help them along as we all struggle to inherit our destiny of freedom, consciousness, and peace.

BEING A WOMAN

I have heard it said that the word "woman" means the "womb of man" or the "womb of the mind." Indeed, in our sacred service as mothers, we are challenged to sculpt the very first impressions upon innocent, tender, malleable human life. For this reason, women must be committed to the very highest values and ideals. Your physiology has evolved to be extremely adept in areas which compliment your role as the mind that is caretaker and nurturer of the miraculous and blessed new products of the womb. The human female brain has evolved into an extremely well-integrated network that allows you to perceive and assess situations very quickly. Our fine-motor abilities allow us to manipulate tiny little things with gentleness and skill. Our psyche has evolved into one that perceives the grave need for humanity to achieve peace and a sacred respect for all. In your naturally beautiful state, you are your husband's most precious validation of his own human excellence, enabling him to see and touch the true meaning of life.

FEMININE PERFECTION

The Prophet Muhammed is said to have described four archetypes as being the four perfect women. The women that he named are: Mary, the mother of Jesus; Asiya, the wife of Pharaoh; Khadijah, the wife of the Prophet Muhammed; and Fatimah, the daughter of the Prophet Muhammed. When the lives of these women are examined, we see a vivid description of four vital characteristic personalities which reside within all women to different degrees or during different phases of life. During your life, you may find yourself expressing these qualities intermittently, with different levels of emphasis at various times. I have found in my marriage that I have inevitably drawn upon the memory of the lives of these women and found myself encouraged and validated by them. I believe that you will equally value reflecting upon these noble women for empowering your own life.

MARY, THE MOTHER OF JESUS

The story of Mary in the Quran actually begins with her own mother, a woman who was a member of the family of Imran, who were themselves descendants of Aaron. The Quran describes the determination of Mary's mother to solemnly dedicate her unborn child to the special service of G-d. When this child is found to be a female child, it is apparently determined that her spiritual service as a female would be very different from the service of a male child, as heard in the Quranic statement that " no male could be like this female." This, and related verses have very powerful implications for clearing up massive misconceptions about the spiritual nature of the human female. They serve as a way of pointing to the unique value of the female physiology. Only a female could have been used to illustrate the magnificent miracle of human conception and birth in the striking way that Jesus' conception and birth did.

Mary also serves as a medium, enabling us to see the human female as being spiritually equal to males because she was the recipient of revelation, as was the mother of Moses. Mary's story further forces us to see that one of G-d's greatest messengers and prophets was born through a woman without any aide from male human physiology. If humankind previously had any doubt as to woman's ability to ascend as a member of the universal soul, Mary's story most certainly serves as a powerful source of enlightenment in this regard. With this, humanity is guided away from thinking that a woman's mind or soul is somehow different from a man's. Rather, G-d seems to be suggesting that it is only our physiological differences that significantly alter the types of earthly duties we are best suited to perform.

We are invited to see that the bodies of men and women are not simply different in their ability to bear children. The Quran clearly suggests that men possess unique physical and physiological abilities that enable them to carry out the challenging duties associated with the physical and psychological work of disseminating, spreading, and establishing the word of G-d. Interestingly, the Quran describes Jesus as being a "word" from G-d. Could this point to a richer meaning and value for the spiritual service that women collectively perform as mothers? Indeed, some might deem the vital and blessed gift of procreation as being the most fundamental form of "revelation." Further, it seems that, perhaps just as women's bodies are uniquely designed for birthing and lactation, men's bodies are better designed for giving forth the conceptual word of G-d, specifically when they must challenge a prevailing male power structure to do so.

It is now known that the male brain is "hardwired" to be very capable of handling great mental stress, solving complex puzzles, navigating successfully through unfamiliar terrain, and dealing with the aggressive tendencies of other males. We can certainly appreciate G-d's abundant mercy and wisdom in sparing females— who serve as the guardians and nurturers of helpless infants and children—from this type of spiritual service. This is reinforced especially when we consider that those men who were charged with establishing G-d's word often suffered grave physical and psychological persecution.

Mary's life also resonates with the value and respect for the role of mothering and motherhood as heard in the Quran's vivid description of Mary's painful labor while birthing Jesus. Our awareness that Mary experienced the severe pains of childbirth is a monumental blessing for all women. With this, G-d soundly undermines the myths that claim that the pains of birth are some sort of punishment against women for encouraging Adam to sin in the garden—this myth is clearly not supported in the Quran. With the birth of Jesus through his mother Mary, we are invited to remember that birth pains are simply the prelude to the arrival of G-d's great mercies in blessing us with precious offspring who are to be cherished and valued.

Women the world over appreciate the story of Mary, the mother of Jesus. There is timeless value to be found in her life and her story has served to purify how we see women in relationship to G-d. Mary is a symbol of the human being's innate spiritual value and the spiritual equality of women. Mary's story is also one that improves our value for the sacred service of motherhood. We can see that the simple desire of a mother to serve G-d with her unborn child was rewarded in a manner that blessed all of humanity. Indeed, it seems that a mother's simple, humble prayer was the impetus for Jesus' birth and great works.

We as women are often called upon to embrace our unique purpose as Mary did at some time in our lives. Mary's humility in accepting her unique challenge is also a special sign for women as we engage in performing our special sacred service, such as childbearing, in areas where G-d has ordained that our husbands cannot travel along with us. With Mary's story, we are invited to walk faithfully through these circumstances in humility, love, and trust.

Allow Mary to represent the part of yourself that is skilled at preserving the inner sanctuary of your spirit and that is reserved for the worship of G-d alone. This is the trusting soul that is resolutely calm and at peace in the accomplishment of her special, inspired life-purpose, even while suffering ridicule from those who simply cannot understand. Know that you can always retreat into a safe spiritual refuge that shelters you in the awareness that G-d is firmly in charge.

ASIYA, THE WIFE OF PHARAOH

The story of Asiya is scant in the Quran yet she is described as the woman who saved Moses when he was found drifting upon the waters in a basket. Asiya intuitively sensed that this child of mystery would be a source of good to her household. Indeed, the good that Moses brought was an extremely powerful movement that served to liberate an entire nation for the worship of the One G-d. Asiya is also known to have accepted the logic of monotheism over the culture and religion of the oppressive Pharaoh, although Pharaoh commanded enormous political power in addition to being her husband.

Asiya's remarkable story is one of sincerity, honor, and great courage. Asiya was also obviously a woman of great intuition and logic. It is sometimes said that Pharaoh did away with her for her betrayal. Interestingly, the Quran does not even mention this event. Rather, we are given only a very comforting depiction of G-d's value for Asiya's service to humanity. Whether or not her demise occurred that way, Asiya's awareness of the great possibility that she might face her death by affirming her belief in One G-d, apparently did not dissuade her. As a demonstration of her willingness to forego the material benefits of being the wife of Pharaoh, she prayed exclusively to G-d, asking G-d to erect a mansion in Paradise for her in nearness to Him.

Asiya's story invites us to understand the great value that G-d places upon women who stand up for what is true and right so as to liberate the souls of the oppressed. Her story yields a sense that we can successfully endure tremendous amounts of stress when we are surrendering totally to G-d. Asiya's character is reflected in those aspects of ourselves that cannot stand to see any human being suffering. Most importantly, her life speaks to the self that accepts being the mother to children although they are not borne of her own womb. Throughout history, special women have shared their lives with children in this way, serving to

29

preserve the lives of orphaned children and entire communities during harsh times.

Asiya's struggles certainly do address the lives of women who find themselves married to severely oppressive men, yet her story also speaks to the condition of oppression that entire societies or communities find themselves facing at times. The oppression of decent families by efforts that seek to protect commercial interests at all costs and at the expense of sacred human life-essence can be seen as a manifestation of a Pharaoh-like paradigm. As women and mothers, we are challenged continuously to overcome the effects of senseless violence, addictive patterns of behavior, escapism and empty sexuality, while striving to preserve the precious value of human life as we give much needed support to those efforts which seek to provide children with positive self-esteem and a sound education.

Like Asiya, as women we are challenged within our communities to find the moral courage to "speak truth to power" especially on behalf of the protection of needy children, when circumstance calls us forth. We are blessed to know that G-d prizes the works and lives of such efforts and that He blesses them with eternal honor and security.

KHADIJAH, THE WIFE OF MUHAMMED

The Lady Khadijah, known to all Muslims as "Mother of the Faithful," was the first person to convert to the Islamic faith in support of the mission of our Prophet Muhammed. Prior to being commissioned as the last prophet sent to mankind, Muhammed served as Khadijah's employee, the dutiful father to her children, and her loyal and devoted husband. Her marriage to Muhammed was filled with tranquility and love and lasted for twenty-five years; until Khadijah passed away. We can see enormous significance in Khadijah's demonstration of the use of her powerful sensibilities. She exemplified a pristine trust in

G-d, and also perfect trust in her husband. After the first traumatic experience of receiving the revelation of scripture, Muhammed was stricken with fear and confusion as to the meaning of the strange spiritual episode. It was Khadijah's resolve that grounded and comforted her husband. She assured Muhammed that he was not losing his mental faculties by engaging her tools of simple clear judgment and logic.

Khadijah wisely advised her husband that G-d would not cause a man of his character to suffer. She reasoned that G-d would hardly cause a man having the utmost integrity, humility and honor, to be mentally incapacitated in such a harsh way. Khadijah's keen perceptions revealed a most beautiful ability to appreciate the natural relationship that we are always striving to have with G-d. Muhammed was nursed and comforted by his dutiful wife, and then she took him to consult with the most valid religious mind that she could find. The consultation with the Christian monk, Waraqa ibn-Nawfal—Khadijah's cousin—served to validate Khadijah's own instinctive awareness. Waraqa further advised them both that Muhammed was the anticipated prophet and messenger of G-d who was foretold in the previous scriptures. He warned Muhammed that his mission would be one that would likely be characterized by great hardship and persecution.

Even with this expectation of future hardship, Khadijah didn't abandon or discourage her husband; instead, she wholeheartedly practiced the tenets of the Islamic faith. Although Khadijah did endure great sacrifices due to her decision, she always provided great financial support and comfort to Muhammed as well as to the early Muslim converts. She also used her vast wealth to aide the new Muslim community, especially for purchasing the freedom of slaves.

While the latter years of Khadijah's life certainly provide us with the greatest sense as to her magnificent character, we are also aware that the Lady Khadijah had been a keen entrepreneur and a shrewd businesswoman. In her earlier years, she successfully identified Muhammed as possessing those qualities that would make him a great employee. Thus, she hired him to serve as her lead trader. Later, Khadijah pursued Muhammed, through an intermediary, for her husband.

We also know of Khadijah that, during the years when idolatry was prevalent in Mecca, she did not participate in the practices of idolatry. She is considered to be among the *Hunafa*—those who did not participate in pagan rituals and practices even before Muhammed's mission ensued. This reveals the character of a woman who possessed an independent mind, while holding herself accountable to her own G-d given sensibilities.

We exhibit the qualities of Khadijah when we lovingly assist our husbands as wife-partners. We are also operating in this role when we shore up our love's awareness of himself in his most favorable characteristics. With this, we exhibit the womanly skill of providing an accurate mirror of a man's excellent value even when his own mind seems to doubt. We are expressing ourselves as Khadijah when we are applying sound logic to any situation and when we are responsibly carrying out our sacred duties. We are also Khadijah when we are enduring hardship and isolation, while our husbands struggle on our behalf and on behalf of pursuing great and meaningful goals.

Khadijah's maturity invites us to welcome into our spirit a voice that is seasoned, savvy, and confident. It is the voice of our own mothers and grandmothers when they are imparting to us the wisdom of the ages. It is also the voice of the assertive lover, the excellent companion, and the skillful entrepreneur who is woman enough to know how to successfully court the man of her dreams. Khadijah was the quintessential wife: perceptive, honest, trustworthy and, above all, a loyal servant of G-d. Khadijah was also most gratefully blessed to be wed to a wonderfully strong, honest, kind, gentle, and intelligent wise-man, one who just happened to be some fifteen years younger than she, as well as the messenger of G-d.

FATIMAH, THE DAUGHTER OF MUHAMMED

The relationship between Muhammed and his daughter Fatimah is regarded as being very loving and warm. Fatimah was a devout Muslim, a devoted wife and mother, and a loving daughter. It is said that Fatimah was the apple of her father's eye. The delightful friendship that Fatimah enjoyed with her father was eclipsed only by the loyalty that she had for his mission. Fatimah made Muhammed laugh and vice versa; she also seemed to bring out the boyish side of him. It is known that on at least one occasion, as a married woman, Fatimah took her complaints to her father. Muhammed then stood up for her, defending her verbally, just as any doting father would. We also see that when Muhammed was dying, he took great care to be with his Fatimah to comfort her and to make her laugh.

The bond that girls have with their fathers is very special. Even as a wife and mother you will realize that there is a part of a girl's heart that belongs only to daddy. He is your guardian and your friend, and he is the voice of strength that reminds husbands that they are caring for a precious soul who is cherished tremendously as someone's darling little girl.

Like Fatimah, we should know when to seek out a father's advisements or intervention in our marriage as a father is always his daughter's trusted Guardian-Advisor—*Wali*. Fatimah's life also reminds us that even when girlish days are far behind us, there is an aspect of girl-spirit that should always be alive as a vital part of our womanly personality. We must strive to keep this part of ourselves in good health and spirits. As wives we are never to forget how to have fun with our love. The Fatimah-inspired girl-spirit enjoys life, play, and humor and is ever appreciative of the chance to explore vast and new discoveries. She admires and trusts in her husband's strengths and inherent genius without reservation, just as a girl innocently admires and trusts in her father. Yet she also knows when to stand up for herself just as any little girl knows just the right way to make her demands known.

My own girl-spirit has kept me smiling at my husband even when I know I probably could be as mad as anything. It is the voice that says, "Oh, he is such a silly boy," rather than declaring, "I hate that horrible man!" It is that part of me that knows that I too am still growing, evolving, and learning, and not to take any of it all too seriously. The girl-spirit even knows how to complain in a way that makes a man feel happy and strong rather than debilitated and overwhelmed.

I have found that we as women have lost so much of our little girl selves that we sometimes become sick and tired, despite still being chronologically very young. The little girl spirit is one that keeps us aware of our immaturity, basic desires and primal fears. The woman in touch with this aspect of herself is not ashamed to be human because she hasn't yet been taught to be so. She has not yet been taught to lie about things that are true, even when she is feeling vulnerable and afraid. The Fatimah-inspired woman invites the man in her life to want very much to care for her, because she is precious to him in her innocent beauty. She inspires in him a protective love as he instinctively seeks to preserve that aspect of human life that is innocent and tender. Fatimah-inspired womanhood is always ready to be grateful, wide-eyed and joyous and is always willing to forgive and renew.

LOVE

I cannot truly say that I know yet what love is. I am still discovering love's persona and gradually understanding its presence. As I live, make mistakes and find myself renewed and more whole, I feel a deep sense of love from G-d. Perhaps this is what makes the loving of my husband more meaningful. This love that I hold for him has developed over many years: it is very different from how I felt about him in the beginning, but I believe that this is love.

When I was a new bride I loved more than anything how my husband made me feel about myself. I craved his endorsements of my intelligence, my beauty or my abilities. I still cherish his validations tremendously, but I have had to accept that there are times that I am not the smartest or the prettiest or the most capable at performing some task in his eyes. Moreover, we have lived together long enough for him to experience my company when I am not in the very best of moods.

While I am no longer fed continuous reflections of my delightfulness, I love far more now than I could ever have had the capacity to love in earlier years. It is difficult to describe but you develop a deep caring about your husband that is present, even when you go through those moments when you do not *like* him for whatever reason. You begin to see his beautiful soul, as well as his good intentions for his family and his fellow man, more than you see any other aspect of him. Love-filled tears may creep into your eyes when you think about his innocent heart and you see beyond his presence as flesh. You come to see him in his essence and in his goodness. You feel bound to help the essential self residing within him to survive and thrive in any way that you can, even when you and he are experiencing wintry days. You are bound by your humanity, and you simply cannot stop caring about him.

FEMININITY
Your feminine self is a gift to all of humanity. Femininity is essentially the outer manifestation of the mind of the womb. Whether you are aware of it or not, a very strong reason for your man-love's attraction to you is that you are radiating the qualities of this womb-spirit continuously.

The womb is a warm, protective and perfectly nurturing environment that expands as its cargo grows. The womb supplies nutrition and comfort: it is also filled with invisible layers of mystery. It is true that there are some husbands who become so accustomed to the womb's protection and security that they are reluctant to take leave of its safe boundaries. Yet, the womb also remembers how to safely expel its cargo with great and consistent force when the command of G-d wills it to do so. When we interact with our love we are always relating some message as to whether we will allow him to enjoy this wonderful escape from the masculine world into this special, loving space.

While we have learned that, in part, femininity is captured in the wearing of fine clothes, lovely fragrances and elegant jewelry, these things should be experienced as being only the bright reflections that radiate light from the spirit of true femininity. The feminine spirit is most authentically the spirit that seeks to preserve and respect all life. The feminine spirit is filled with appreciation for The Creator of all living things and, especially, it is the spirit that cherishes the lives of babies born in every hue and color. You will surely magnetize your man to your womb with the shimmers and sparkles of jewels, the fragrances of rare flowers, and your silken-velvets cast in alluring colors, but do not forget to remember that you are regaled in your most feminine attire when you are inspiring among men the sacred love and respect that human beings should hold for one another.

YOUR GARDEN

I have heard it said that everything in the natural world has some expression within the human soul. I know that I have felt the heat of the desert deep down within my belly, although never actually setting foot on its hot sand. I have also felt the cold Arctic winds breathing from the lips of another human being. In all extremes of climate, terrain, and weather, I strive to maintain the most vivid descriptions of the natural world as found in scripture... these being the descriptions of the paradise for the human spirit described to us as being a magnificent garden. The Quran reminds us continuously of the garden as being our first and final home. Perhaps G-d uses this description to give us focus because no other setting offers human beings more solace or spiritual rest than do gardens.

As a young bride, you will likely cultivate your garden among a great deal of external things. This is exactly as it should be. Yet, do not neglect to cultivate as well, the garden within your mind and spirit, daily. Stop to give thanks and praise for this amazingly awesome life experience. Think about sweet life and the hope for a color-filled, satisfying, eternal future. Set up your fountains as you give selfless love to your husband, respecting him as G-d's servant and property. Plant your flowers and evergreens as you serve your fellow man and assist your neighbor. Make your garden fragrant with mists of oils that you have pressed from fruit skins picked from full trees that are planted each and every time you do something good, simply because you know that G-d is seeing.

WEDDING DAY
Excitement and anticipation are all experienced fully in this all-too-quickly-moving moment in time; marking the end and the beginning. This day, so anticipated, goes so fast. Jubilant exhaustion, frozen smiles, and tears of love and joy flow from many understanding eyes. You hope to find one or two special moments when you are able to suspend the flow and just talk to G-d about all of these things—about gratitude and love, about His marvelous design, and also about private new galaxies that are yet to be explored.

THE MAN THAT YOU LOVE
It took me some time to grasp the understanding that men are very different from women in rather significant ways. I

am now aware that most men process information from a slightly different perspective; they also have different sensitivities than we do. Of course, there is no single "man" prototype that fits all men. However, the similarities among men are manifested with strong consistency across race, religion, and culture. Like women, men share certain common sensitivities that are a by-product of physiological differences in their hormonal orchestra and in the way their brains process stimuli.

Males have evolved with unique patterns that seem to be very much tied to their high instincts for providing food and protection for their families. These patterns may seem odd in today's world yet, seen in the backdrop of anthropological development, we certainly do understand.

Like women, men have various propensities and archetypes which most men seem to share, with some aspects of these tendencies expressing themselves more overtly than others. Your own husband may primarily be a hunter, focused on providing food and a sense of material security. This is often the most prized expression of masculinity as it provides for our fundamental survival needs. The most vivid modern view of this male is as the "maverick" businessman. Sometimes, we see extreme expressions of him as the "workaholic."

Alternatively, your husband may primarily be a tribesman, having a very strong propensity for procreation, thus ever expanding his tribe. These men are obviously very sexually motivated.

Your love may have a strong expression of his military general personality, demonstrating a strong need to lead his "troops" so as to be prepared for possible attacks, wars, or some type of hostile invasion if necessary. These men can come across as commanding and overbearing. Yet, when understood in the proper context, one can value this strong energy for domination as being tied to a strong will to protect the women, children, and community that he deeply cares so much about.

Most men also have somewhere inside of them a youthful boy, the fun or playful companion who is always ready for an adventure. In addition, men can possess the unique qualities of visionary father. This quality is a highly evolved aspect of a man's nature, one that understands the need for humanity to have the greatest opportunity for survival as a group. This visionary aspect in men is very spiritually grounded. It can be expressed as a wise, reflective leader who is devoted to creating optimal circumstances for peace among mankind as a whole, as well as within his home. Some men who seem to be soft-spoken are often in this highly evolved category. They can be mistaken for being weak, while they are really extremely strong insofar as being able to protect the tribe from long term and far-reaching harm by using their G-d given sensibilities to the maximum.

As with women, the dominant types are expressed to various degrees in different men. In some cases, one aspect seems to over-dominate. If this is the case, we may see a man that is considered "not well adjusted." Often women tend to fantasize about the perfect husband in ways that have integrated all of these aspects with some degree of balanced expression. It is interesting to note that the Prophet Muhammed seemed to possess all of these qualities in a perfect balance. It is likely that, on any given day, you will see several of these personalities working within your husband as well.

Rather than to discount your love because he dominates more in some areas, you should cherish, value, and praise him for those areas that G-d has inspired him to develop strongly. You can also experiment in fun ways by inviting other aspects of his personality to come out. Value his strengths and allow them to compliment yours. Remember that when motivated by love and respect for your husband's humanity, you are always in the strongest position for experiencing all of the best in him.

SERVING HIM

We often have such deeply embedded sensitivities about servitude and service, especially when this involves being in the service of men. We fear subservience and being dominated or perhaps being looked down upon by other women who consider themselves as having become liberated from oppressive roles of the past. I think, however, that you will find a special kind of joy in serving and caring for your husband; that is, if he is indeed the man that you love. If your husband is demanding and likes to pretend to be a five star general, there are several fun ways to rein him in. This should not be a cause for you to abandon the delicate art of giving care to him. Truly, in serving any human being we are serving G-d. Interestingly, we are sometimes more capable of serving the needs of our sister-friends, children, or parents, than those of our own husband. This can be remedied by reminding oneself that charity begins at home and within.

Give your gentle care, not expecting anything in return and simply as a means of earning blessings and forgiveness from G-d. You will find that your nurturing makes him more capable of transcending. You might like to think of your gentle care as the fuel that feeds his massive rocket engines, allowing him to propel you both into the heavens. In your regular acts of humble service, you are also providing him with an invisible, mighty anchor, as well as a homing device that will be always pulsing through his heart and psyche as it gently guides him back home.

Love him knowing that he is G-d's servant and a blessed gift to your family. You will undoubtedly find that your love and caring will imbue your entire home with a beautiful energy and spirit. Also remember—if and when he offers to serve you kindly in any small way—to accept his gestures with a simple smile and a sincere "thank you."

For Sakinah

THE GOOD DEED

I met Tariqa early one Saturday morning as my brother and I were dropping off my eldest son to spend the week away at Boy Scout camp. She appeared to be in her mid to late fifties but she had a girlish spirit and a warm smile. With her grandson in tow, Tariqa approached me to ask a favor. After she dropped off her grandson she needed someone to chauffeur her around for the day so that she could tend to some very urgent family business. I was capable of helping out, yet I had some apprehension. I didn't know her at all and the favor required that some degree of trust be employed. Tariqa said that she'd taught for some time at a local Islamic school and she mentioned several people that I knew, who could vouch for her character. I called my husband to ask his advice and he approved of the venture while insisting that I take my brother along with me as a precaution. At the end of the day, Tariqa invited us to have dinner in her lovely and beautifully furnished home. She served us graciously and generously using her finest china, lace tablecloth and napkins. That evening Tariqa did everything that she could to show us that she was grateful for our small act of kindness. Looking back, I know that I could not have made a better investment than I did that day. I spent one day doing a small favor for someone who, over the years, would return the kindness many times over; Tariqa became so much more to me than a friend.

As it turned out, Tariqa was also a nurse and she was raising her grandson by herself. With all that she had to manage, she somehow found the time to be one of the truest friends that I have ever known. She was the type of "sister" who would come to your home and clean it up if you were sick or if you were simply feeling overwhelmed. She offered encouragement at every turn and we always traded advice as to what the best method of keeping something clean or organized was. Since the day that I met her, she was always there for me. She picked up my children from school, sometimes cooked dinner for my family, made us laugh and educated us as to what was going on in the world from her very seasoned perspective. On one occasion, after being discharged from the hospital with a newborn baby, Tariqa warmly opened her home to my family and me while we completed some remodeling on our home. She was also largely responsible for my being able to make the pilgrimage to Mecca, as she lovingly cared for my seven children and my niece for three weeks while we were away. I never worried about them. I trusted that she was taking care of them just as I would have—perhaps even a bit better.

When I think about my friend, I think of the Quranic verse where G-d informs us that when we spend our resources in His cause, our investment grows like a grain of corn that multiples many times over. Tariqa's humble friendship exemplified this principle perfectly. I spent one short day doing a small favor for her and, in turn, her friendship became an immeasurable blessing to me. It seems that during the fifteen or so years that I knew her, she was constantly giving, helping, serving and caring for me—always intelligently and ever so graciously. I always tried to out-do my friend as I attempted to provide the same type of favors for her. We kept a sort of competition going on to see who could be the best sister-friend to the other, and who could assist the other through life more selflessly. Looking back, I realize that she was always the victor, for I could never seem to keep up with her high level of love and selfless generosity. What a good person she was...what a good Muslim...what a beautiful sister-friend...and what a lady. I pray often that more women might know the type of friendship that I was gifted with when I was blessed to meet Tariqa.

FRIENDS
Cherish your good friends very deeply, solemnly, and dearly. I cherish with all my heart my beautiful sister-

friends, phenomenal in their giving and humility; superb women in the love that they send forth, which flows out constantly to their parents, husbands, children and also, to me. These lovely spirit-filled ladies have held me, prayed over me, and sometimes they carried me. Yes, it is true; on many days they lifted me up and carried me.

FORGIVE
Please do. Forgive yourself and your love, and any others that you can. Forgive them very much and very, very often.

PLAN TOGETHER
When I was a younger bride, I had absolutely no idea how much planning must go into the business of marriage. Take council together every week or so as to how the business of marriage is running. This small undertaking will serve you immensely especially if you are to have children. At these councils you should establish standards, goals, priorities, duties and, of course, a budget. Decide who will do what chores and when. Assess how things are working periodically. In addition, strive to create the culture of consultation and accountability.

IMPULSES
We all have moments when we are suddenly influenced to do or say something that has a negative effect on those we love. These impulses may come "out of the blue," often while we are not aware. Remember that our speech, gestures, body language and attitudes, are continuously being influenced by television, print media, and film personalities. Sometimes, our friends or relatives influence our actions and we might be completely unaware that they are vibrating a somewhat negative and contagious mood or energy. Try to recognize when your thoughts, actions, or words are not authentically your own. This happens to

most of us so don't be too disappointed in yourself if you see these tendencies crop up from time to time.

Be sure to remember also, that there are always very powerful positive impulses that are constantly being projected through us, those that suggest or invite us to do something kind or good. We can be just as unaware of these potentially healing, whispering voices. The Quran invites us to follow these impulses for doing good. The whisper of any good impulse provides a blessed opportunity to restore and delight the spirits of our loved ones. Take care to listen. You will find that there is always an inner whisper filling your thoughts with ideas of small kindnesses that you can do. Be it a gentle touch, a cup of tea, or a small token that tells him that you are aware of the little things that he likes. Seize these splendid moments of opportunity.

HUMILITY

I think that there is no finer quality to cultivate in one's character than this. Humility is borne of an instinctive awareness that we are all still becoming. Without humility, we would all cease to grow and learn. You will notice that when you are humble, you feel more human and more at ease within your body and spirit. It is wise to recall that in the Quran G-d suggests that the thought "I am better than he" is not native to the human being's truest self. It can be challenging to maintain your humility when you believe that you are smarter, wiser, or more pious than another in some way. However, know also that G-d has given each one of us special gifts. Often, the abilities and gifts that others possess are invisible to our eyes until we have grown inward into other dimensions of understanding.

ANGER

It is said that anger is like fire that destroys everything in its path. I am sadly a witness to this truth. How I wish that I could have known more about curbing my anger as a young bride and at other critical junctures in my life. It is indeed difficult to be spoken to unkindly or treated unjustly. However, anger inevitably clouds and confounds the issues making it that much more difficult to sort things out and make corrections. As I realized that anger is usually the expression of feeling great psychological hurt or fear of being harmed, I have grown increasingly more capable of curbing my anger. I try to allow my inner parent to take an audible "front and center" presence in my moments of psychological and emotional anguish. I state aloud and within myself that "G-d is more real than anything else that I am perceiving." I say this over and over until my thoughts are clear.

If the anger persists, I try to extinguish it again and again. Try saying this out loud before responding to your love in anger. He at least will understand that you are having a really hard time. I cannot encourage you enough to take your hurts to G-d before responding to your love out of anger. If he hurts your feelings, tell G-d on him first. Wait patiently for G-d's instructions before you speak. And try to remember that G-d understands and loves you both.

HITTING

No marriage that I know of has tolerated hitting as a part of its lasting culture. We are, of course, aware that there are very specific Quranic restrictions upon men hitting their wives. These verses only apply to the circumstance of a wife who is believed guilty of some lewd or potentially disloyal behavior. In this case there is a three-stage process that completely negates the super-charged atmosphere that invites males to impulsively strike out at women in rage or anger. If a wife is deemed as having seriously done something that is harmful to the marriage, husbands are exhorted to first offer a verbal warning. Interestingly, this may be sufficient to break the cycle of impulsive male anger because this challenges husbands to use thoughtful communication rather than aggression. The initial verbal warning must then be followed by a refusal to share his wife's bed. This obviously serves as a superb test to see if the husband is really serious about his concerns. And finally, if both of these actions fail—this likely would require the passing of a significant number of days—then a "strike" is permitted. The Arabic word used for strike— *daraba*—is rich with meaning as seen by the numerous ways in which it is used throughout the Quran. Most importantly, the word does not necessarily connote that there be any significant physical contact at all.

With this, G-d makes it virtually impossible for an observant Muslim husband to explode with violence against his wife simply because he has a bad day, or because he may possesses strongly aggressive male tendencies. We are additionally blessed to have as the perfect model human being the Prophet Muhammed, who strongly spoke out against the practice of husbands hitting upon their wives.

Even when a "strike" is technically allowed, the language used in the Quran seems to suggest that men might use strong, vivid words to "strike" with. There is also a subtly implied suggestion that this "strike" might be done with a handful of grass! Some would argue that the best interpretation of "strike," in this context, is for the husband of a wife who is persistently lewd, to distance himself from her by putting her out of the home as the last resort.

While the Quran does not directly restrict women from hitting their husbands, it is unkind and very unwise, even when done playfully, to inflict any sort of physical pain upon the man that you love. Although he may not complain—perhaps not wanting to seem weak—men, similarly to women, do not like to be hit.

LAUGHTER
Laughing together and enjoying one another's humor is one of marriage's purest gems. Even when you are

supposed to be angry, it is really all right to allow some humor to sparkle through.

HARD WORK AND HUMOR

At a recent *Nikkah*—the Islamic ceremony affirming the wedding vows—the officiating Imam wisely informed us all that marriage is hard, hard, hard, hard, hard work! He suggested to the bride and groom that they meet this mighty challenge with "F-A-I-T-H"—using the word as an acronym. He said that the "H" in faith stood for humor. He exhorted the young couple to allow themselves to laugh, as sometimes things would get so difficult that they might have to laugh to keep from crying. We all laughed heartily at these comments and all of the married couples who were present gave their enthusiastic endorsements of this advice with spirited shouts of "that's right!" Just know that it is possible in many instances to find humor in some things rather than designate them as a signal of some major, irreparable marital flaw. This is very often dependent upon previous preconditioning as to what you are anticipating your marriage to be and your willingness to see things from a slightly different perspective.

And do rely on faith as a reflection of the trust that we invest in G-d, as well as the excellence found in everything good that G-d has created.

WIFIN'

Shortly after my dear friend Sabreen had courageously embarked upon her third marriage, she pulled me aside after the Friday *Jumah* Prayer Service. "Listen," she whispered into my ear, "I really need to talk to you. You know I love my new husband terrifically, yet I feel somewhat overwhelmed with adjusting to being in a new marriage." I could tell that, although Sabreen was serious, she was also in a bit of a playful mood. With a hint of a chuckle and a wide smile she asked, "Could you spare some time to talk with me? I could sure use some help with this new wifin' business." We both giggled as I promised my support. My good friend Sabreen has since passed away, but her wise comments have stayed with me. She was older than I was; yet, she was humble enough to seek out help from someone whom she thought could be of assistance. I recognized in her attitude tremendous humility.

Sabreen was a very wise woman possessing great intellect and sound judgment, yet, she was wise enough to also know when she could use some support. She turned to me because she knew that she could trust me completely. I had demonstrated to her in the past that I was a sound confidante and that I would never compromise her privacy. She also knew that I was devoted to strengthening marriages. When in need of this kind of assistance, your mother or sister is likely the person best suited to support you through these times of adjustment. If your mother or sister cannot be there for you, it is all right to seek out the advice of a trusted married friend if she demonstrates excellent character, and is supportive of marriage. One should, of course, still be mindful of preserving one's husband's privacy.

The other lesson that Sabreen taught me was to have fun with the learning curve that all new wives inevitably experience. She didn't waste time belittling herself or blaming her new husband for the growing pains that she was experiencing. In isolating the problems with "wifin'," she simply accepted that, as with any new job, there were new things to learn in a new marriage. In effect, she taught me to accept that, at every stage of life and marriage, I should embrace being a student and not take any of the growth processes all too seriously.

SUCCESS
It is very likely that you will expend a considerable amount of mental energy on becoming "successful." This pursuit can be enormously productive, yet, can also prove to be

enormously disabling. Success is such an emotionally charged concern, often having far more to do with what you think with respect to how others perceive your life accomplishments, rather than with how *you* perceive them. It is only natural for us to want our parents to be satisfied and pleased with our life's choices because we desire that they know that their hard work in rearing us has been rewarded. Still, we can also become so concerned with evaluation by others that we become stagnant as individuals, confined in ways that threaten to discourage us from our unique life's purpose, creativity and individuality.

To some, my choice of devoting my life to the work of wifing and mothering is a loss compared to my earlier stated goals of becoming a pediatrician. Yet, no one besides G-d and I can understand the delight and sense of deep fulfillment I enjoy as a result of my career decision. Interestingly, it seemed that when others finally understood that I had not fallen into the life's work of being a stay at home mom by default, but rather chosen this path intentionally, they seemed to gain a certain respect for me. Even after becoming a registered professional nurse, I continued to respond that I was a homemaker when questioned as to my chosen vocation. To this end, I have found that when we are comfortable with ourselves and our life choices, others inevitably become comfortable with them. I also understood that people's perceptions as to our success ultimately reflects how we are feeling about who we are within ourselves.

STANDING YOUR GROUND
In marriage, as in life, there are matters about which you must firmly stand your ground. Our loyalty must always be to G-d's guidance and to what rests within our conscience. During these times, remember that standing one's ground can be done quietly and sensitively without hurting feelings or making a fuss. You can humbly ask your love to understand and to forgive you for any difficulty that your

position may be causing him. As with so many things, when executed with humility, the end results are more satisfying. Essentially, I have found that standing one's ground is best accomplished when you are psychologically "seated."

INTIMACY
Refined ladies take care to keep their special play-lessons as intimately private, musical sessions.

RELAXATION
It is difficult to relax when one does not know the outcome. We human beings are inevitably and instinctively always seeking to avoid discomfort. When we are able to trust G-d's ultimate plan and perfect love for us, we can relax. Release and relaxation is accomplished through paying attention to those aspects of oneself that are habitually contracting or tensing-up in anticipation of physical or psychological discomfort. Trust in your G-d, my love. He has not created you to harm you.

SISTER MARY
One of my elder sister-friends, Sister Mary, pulled me aside one day, her face revealing a very serious mood. "You know sister, when Allah tells the men-folk that they will have all of these virgins in paradise, He is really talking about us! Yes, sister, some say that they will each have up to seventy two!" I was a bit surprised with Sister Mary's selected topic for discussion, as she and I had never discussed such matters before. She continued, "Sister, Allah is telling us that He is going to renew us all. He is going to purify all of the righteous women in mind, in body and in spirit!" By now her serious mood had turned to one filled with excitement. She declared her final news to me with joy. "Sister, we are going to be renewed as virgins, again, and again, and again." She went on as if trying to pull me up to a plateau far above us, upon some

high ground that she had somehow secretly attained. "Isn't this wonderful?" she asked, her eyes lit with joy and contentment as she conveyed these newly discovered ideas.

Sister Mary further explained that virginity was really a state of mind and a state of being. When senses and sensitivities were pure and not dulled by preconceived notions, excessive external stimuli, or unnecessary shame, we are as virgins. She said that, in today's culture, many who have never been sexually active are so over-exposed to sexual imagery and cultural influences that they are gradually losing their virgin-purity within their spirits and within their psyche. Sister Mary assured me, however, that with focused concentration and the discipline of modesty, one could learn to preserve one's innocent sensitivities.

ALL SEVENTY-TWO
Each one and more are right there inside of you; purified, wide eyed and sanctified!

CELEBRATE
Make time to celebrate with your love regularly. These celebrations need not cost a lot of money. Celebrate life and your union in some small way as a regular tradition. Inviting friends over to share in your energy can be very nice as well. In doing so, you provide the community with an opportunity to socialize in a safe setting while sharing in the joy of your union.

HIS SPECIAL ENERGY
I believe that men experience a sort of parallel world with us women. While we do share in the same desires and goals and dreams, men also seem to have their own private world that, in many ways, we seem barred from entering. They seem to have their own rules and sensitivities. In some ways, men's instincts are more developed than our own—and in some things, our instincts seem to be more

so. In creating us as compatible mates, G-d has given us a marvelously complimentary design that serves and benefits all if we yield to its beauty and sensibility.

When I was growing up, I was sometimes told by women, outright, that men were simply not intelligent or that they behaved "just like animals." The women who were imparting these messages often had been subjected to tragic spousal abuse. Therefore, their worlds offered up somewhat skewed information as to how to understand, value, and get along with good men. I was blessed, however, to have been reared by a devoted and loving grandfather. Thanks to him, I knew that men could be wise, responsible, courageous, kind, intelligent, creative, strong, industrious, gentle, and G-d fearing. I have now come to see that life challenges men in slightly different ways than it challenges women. Indeed, science bears this out in many ways.

The most vivid scientific example of this fact is evident when we study the effects of testosterone upon the male. With this hormone, G-d has placed within the male physiology the powerful drive to procreate, thus keeping the human race successfully populating the earth. While high levels of testosterone have been a monumental blessing to human life, testosterone is also a great trial for men. We can only try to imagine the benefits of this powerful elixir in the life of early man. A primitive man might be faced with the challenge of guarding his wife, perhaps just after having birthed a newborn baby, from a lion prowling at the vault of their cave. He was surely in need of very high levels of this survival hormone. From an anthropological view, one can see that men's aggressive tendencies have always served a very important purpose. However, in today's world, we see many men faltering under the powerful influence of testosterone as they pursue sex, domination, or violence irresponsibly.

Due to this fact, women sometimes find it challenging not to slip into the pattern of prejudging the men they love because of the wounds that other women have experienced. Rather than focusing on the disruptive aspects of the male energy, when you look at your love try to remember that this same powerful male energy has gifted him with the ability to apply intense amounts of focus towards solving innumerable, serious problems which have challenged the human race. Indeed, men are responsible for bringing enormous progress to our species.

Your ability to value the great benefits that the vital masculine presence has brought to humanity will become exponentially more important if you are blessed to become the mother of a son. To assist them in harnessing their natural testosterone-inspired abilities, we should remind our sons that we are gifted with countless aspects of progress and modernity because of this special, blessed, manly energy. Among the special gifts given to us by men are bridges, automobiles, airplanes, new medicines, computers, infinite technological things, mass production and distribution methods, institutions of higher learning and also, political systems that strive to serve and promote the dignity of man.

We know as well, that the world has suffered great human loss and destruction as a result of misdirected energy unleashed by men. Yet, while we know that men have started many wars, we must also appreciate that other men fight wars reluctantly and only to protect the cherished lives of their women and their children. As your marriage unfolds, be observant as to what ideas are influencing your expectations and perceptions about the man that you love. In addition, try to appreciate that we all have been blessed dearly as a result of his special masculine energy.

FEELING TAKEN FOR GRANTED

At some point, you will likely feel taken for granted. At times, your love will likely feel this way as well. Hopefully, you both won't feel these feelings at the same time. When this timing conflict does occur, there is an opportunity for the fabric of your relationship to be weakened. The funny thing is that these times can, conversely, provide the opportunity for your relationship to be strengthened. Rather than to allow emotional divisions to take root; you can employ a few safe strategies.

First, don't waste precious energy with scorekeeping. There is no legitimate way of registering or weighing how many nice or giving acts you have done for your husband versus how many nice or good things he has done for you. We know that from the Islamic perspective, good deeds are done for the pleasure of G-d and not so that we might be rewarded by another person. This is heard in the caution that we should not cancel out our good deeds with reminders. In effect, when we keep score of our good deeds we are putting dynamics in place that can potentially cause injury. Another strategy we can utilize is to provide him with some of the nurturing he is craving and then let him know what nurturing you need from him. This is offered in the spirit of the reported saying of our Prophet who advised that we be honest and forthright with one another going directly to the root of the problem.

Now, if you are thinking "That's not fair. Why should I give in first? I am always the one giving," then you are keeping score again! Keep in mind that offering him something special need not mean that you prepare a six-course gourmet meal. Rather, it may simply mean that you are more present for him mentally, that you take the time to notice him, or that you remind him what a great man he is and that you are still so very much in love with him.

A NEW CHILD
If and when a child arrives, you are suddenly and most certainly a newly birthed human being. Also, inevitably and eternally, you are a brand new expression of the universal soul and will never be quite the same as you were before you became a mother. This is a joyous metamorphosis.

Yet, it is sometimes briefly accompanied by tickles of loss and even of sadness as you adjust to giving up some of the life you have become accustomed to. It is far more likely, though, that you will not even notice the little gaps in your life, as your magical child seamlessly fills the spaces and previously unknown voids in ways that your best fantasies could never before have grasped or imagined.

JUGGLING

Like most women with children, if I were to join the circus, I am sure that I would be a phenomenon! This is due to the significant skill that I have developed at juggling. When listed out on paper even I cannot believe all the things for which I am responsible. My husband always wisely advises that I prioritize. Before the children came, this was much easier—but now the priorities have developed layers and levels and categories. It is enough to unravel the strongest of minds! One day I asked my husband, "If you were forced to choose whether you would prefer a perfectly clean house, perfectly ordered children, a perfectly prepared meal, or your wife welcoming you home beautified, rested, and serene within, which would you choose?" Without hesitating, he picked the latter. He said that more than anything in the world, he wanted me to feel contented and strong. He added that my wholeness and happiness were far more valuable to him than anything else that I'd mentioned. So now, when I am tempted to ascend onto the high-wire while balancing four or eight or sixteen spheres launched into the air, I practice snatching out the one that says, "a peaceful and beautiful *me.*" I then remember my husband's kind and loving words and I practice listening to them.

MOM UNIVERSITY

If you are blessed to become a mother, you will need to draw from knowledge in virtually every discipline in order to adequately provide your children with proper care, nutrition, safety, stimulation and education. Motherhood, though sometimes a seemingly "default" profession, in truth, requires vast amounts and varieties of knowledge and accurate information. If you are not doing so already, begin to embrace the lifelong duty of reading everything and anything related to the living of a productive life.

One of the most powerful legacies that Al-Islam has bequeathed to us is that of placing great emphasis upon the pursuit of useful education. Muhammed continuously inculcated into his followers the requirement that we become educated and that we accept responsibility for teaching others. It is most notable that our prophet spent a great deal of energy encouraging males to educate their women-folk. In fact, it is surprising that the prophet Muhammed is not widely celebrated as being *the* most formidable champion of women's rights that history has known. I say this because his traditions regarding the education and treatment of women are unmatched. What historical figure could any one point to that has done more to encourage equality, education and fair treatment for women than he? And what a wise endeavor this was, for it is clear that the progress of any society correlates to the level at which it succeeds in educating and improving the lives of women. Your role as first educator makes you the most important teacher and scholar.

Our prophet Muhammed advised that we embrace knowledge as if knowledge was ones' lost possession. With this in mind, you will likely soon find that wifing and motherhood education encompasses virtually everything from pregnancy, birthing, lactation, nutrition and food science to home and financial management, first aid, psychology and so much more. Hopefully, your academic education will have primed your journey with the basic principles of, and an appreciation for: reading, math, science, literature, philosophy, social sciences/world studies and different languages. And while all of these are truly important, you will find that the most important education is found in that which helps us to hold on to our humanity. These connections are best supplied and preserved through the study of scripture with a focus on hearing those messages that are best suited to unite and bring peace to all people.

Today, leading educators are acknowledging that the days have passed when the achievement of an academic degree at any level can mark the end of schooling. It seems that we have moved into becoming a world where the advice of Muhammed to "seek knowledge from the cradle to the grave" is becoming a reality. We are now in a world where learning must continue as long as we are alive. Furthermore, the language of science, math and technology is rapidly becoming the new basis of true literacy. For this reason, women must embrace education and hold the need for excellent education before our community as a primary need. It is critical that we place great emphasis upon math and science education in particular if we are to help our children to thrive in this new world. If you have the notion that becoming a wife and mother will provide you with some sort of vacation or time out from schooling and learning, get ready for the reality check of a lifetime! Your education has only just begun.

FAMILIES

Marriage unites two families. Therefore, the union that you and your love have created is serving to bind all of humanity together just a bit closer. It is up to both you and your love to strengthen these bonds through kindness, service, humility, and sincere words. Always remember that your husband's family is an extension of him. Try to love them as openly and sincerely as you do him. Especially, take care to nurture the love, honor and respect that you have for his mother, just as you would hope that your own son's wife would value you. Never speak negatively about his mother to him or to anyone—even if your husband does so. If something about your husband's mother is the source of psychological pain, speak about her to G-d. Ask G-d to guide you towards a solution or to the words that will give you both more reasons to strengthen this precious bond. Pray often for G-d's assistance and continue to demonstrate kindness, patience, and good character. While this may be very difficult at first, this investment will pay off generously.

BUYING MILK

When I see a container of low-fat milk in the refrigerator that I myself did not purchase, I become filled with the strongest romantic sensations. You see, no one else in my home drinks milk besides me. We have a very large family so the arrival of milk is somewhat of an oddity. With this ordinary purchase, costing only a few dollars, my love binds my heart to his, firmly and anew. Gifts of chocolate, though delectable, somehow suggest that the giver be compensated with some kind of reward. Gifts of jewelry are wonderful; yet, these prizes can also be so very political. These gifts are sometimes used to present an image for others to view, serving as a sort of public confirmation, or proof, that a wife is loved or that one's husband is thus, loving. However, a new container of milk is so private and special and sincere. The simple cardboard or plastic container speaks that my husband's love is caressing me. With this quiet act he says, "Darling, when I am about my days, be assured that I am thinking special, private, caring thoughts about you."

DESIRES

The Quran makes us realize that every human desire is born of some natural and healthy expression. Indeed, our desires are a gift given to us by G-d. We must take care, however, to nurture our desires while accepting that we are to pursue them in the right way; if we are truly to enjoy the end results of these pursuits with lasting pleasure. We should first take care that our desires are checked by reason, so that we do no harm to our selves. Additionally, in pursuit of our desires, we should seek never to harm another person.

CHALLENGES

In marriage, you will likely work extremely hard with your body, mind, heart, and spirit. Remember always that this work is strengthening you in invisible ways. You are strengthened also when you embrace the challenges of life, rather than seeking to run away from them.

DECORATING

Never wait to start to decorate. Begin creating a beautiful environment for yourself and your love right away. Your home environment does so much to support the presence of good feelings between the two of you. You can complete inexpensive projects making use of good flea markets and upscale thrift stores. And please don't confuse decorating with the act of filling your house with lots of "things." Rather, plan out what accents each space is calling for and then begin working on each area. The foundation of any decorating plan is clean/smooth floors and clean/smooth walls. Paint is a very inexpensive way of transforming the feel of your space. If you are not good with decorating, find a picture of a room that attracts your senses and simply copy it. Think also about the function of your space when you decorate. For example, kitchens need paint that is easily washed and most homes can use furnishing that also provides for storage solutions. A single trip to the library can yield some solid ideas and color schemes which can be applied without much money or extensive time. Remember to utilize color, texture, fabric, light, hues and fragrance to create mood.

For Sakinah

CULTURE OF CLEAN

Clean living is absolutely essential to the Islamic tradition. Along with the ideals of freedom, justice and equality, cleanliness is one of the greatest and most vital distinctions of Islamic culture and the Islamic lifestyle. Muslims view the inherent desire to be clean as one that is native to the original pattern of human creation; we believe that this ideal has vast spiritual implications and significance. In fact, a ritual washing precedes the formal daily prayers that Muslims perform throughout the day. In the early Islamic era, the Muslim community led by the prophet Muhammed, was distinguished because of the diligence they observed towards successfully keeping their bodies, homes and community surroundings clean. In later generations, powerful and beautiful Islamic civilizations flourished having been established upon this principle. As a Muslim woman you are the proud vanguard for this fundamental aspect of Islamic culture, upholding the excellent Islamic standards within your family for cleanliness, order and personal hygiene.

Muslims view cleanliness as a significant aspect of the natural pattern of human nature. Even newborn babies instinctively communicate their displeasure with being unclean as they cry out when they are wet or soiled. Muslims strive to preserve and improve upon this excellent inclination and we have been blessed with scripture that reinforces our commitment to this ideal.

Cleanliness of body and environment is also seen as a metaphor for the cleanliness that we should guard within our minds and spirits. We know that cleanliness is the first step towards preventing the spread of harmful physical diseases but we should also be aware of the connection between cleanliness and the moral foundation that is continuously being established for society. The word "clean" holds the implications of morality, honesty, goodness, justice, clarity, ethics, wholesomeness and that which is plainly evident. Thus, when we cultivate clean living within our homes and among our family members, we are truly laying the foundation for the cultivation of a healthy society for all of humanity.

As standard bearers for this critical aspect of Islamic culture, Muslim women are certainly to be tried and tested. Keeping your home and children in order within our hectic society can be a very significant challenge indeed, however you will find that when your home is clean and ordered, each and every person within your household will enjoy a major psychological advantage. Your diligence in emphasizing this area will powerfully improve your family's ability to think, study, pray, reason and reflect. Also, you will likely find that your marital relationship is less burdened when your home is in order because disorder of any kind can easily influence the spirit negatively. Remember that we have been instructed by G-d and our Prophet Muhammed to keep our bodies, clothing, food, homes and communities very clean and this lifestyle has historically proven to give Muslims a great advantage for living successfully. Whenever Muslims have lost sight of this indispensable value, Islamic community life has suffered tremendously on every level.

WOMAN'S WORK
Yes, I know that it is not politically correct to describe work according to gender. No one knows this better than I, having grown up at the height of the push for equality among American women. The struggle for feminism was brave and certainly necessary; yet, it seems to me that women have somehow lost a great deal along with those things we have gained. For women who have financial means, the feminist movement opened up a smorgasbord of choices. But, for the average woman, those choices were coupled with severe losses. Mothers have become accustomed to carting babies off to day care when they are only a few months old, so they are not threatened with loss of employment. Also, families became comfortable with

the reality that when their children arrive home after school, no one will be there. Furthermore, while we women have certainly demonstrated superior capability at doing the work that men do intellectually, there are few men who are interested in doing the work that women have historically performed. Thus, we are still largely responsible for running the home and managing the care, schedules, and education of our children. Women have proven that we can do it all, but the jury is still out as to whether or not we are yet happy in doing so.

To my disappointment, I have often observed the important discussion of woman's work reduced into some sort of debate that sets mothers who work outside of the home against mothers who choose to stay at home. I believe this debate to be nothing more than a fruitless and ridiculous distraction. The reality is that we, as women, are taking care of the business on all fronts; whether we are working at home or outside, we are all legitimately hard-working women.

Women are simply phenomenal! We are gifted at doing just about everything. We feed, we educate, we defend, we nurse, we serve, we calculate, we entertain, we provide, and we do it all while still feeling ultimately responsible for the duties of running our homes and raising children. And until there is a men's liberation movement that successfully establishes men's rights to perform the home-life duties that women have traditionally done, this reality is simply what it is.

Now, it should be said that, ideally, the Muslim man has already been thus liberated, as our Prophet Muhammed, who is the perfect human model, was the quintessential husband. It is well known and documented that Muhammed did household chores without reservation or remark, right alongside the women. While Muhammed did give clear advisements as to the value of maintaining the vital and elegant human culture of masculine and feminine gender distinctions, he never presented housework as being a distinctly female or feminine role. Amazingly, Muhammed accepted responsibility for home-life duties while also serving as spiritual visionary, head of state, military general, prayer leader, dutiful husband, superb father, ambassador, consultant, and businessman! Muhammed was also relentless in his demands, coercions and invitations for men to be seriously devoted to the education and elevation of their women.

New brides should remember: although they will find that, like most women, they have the amazing ability to fulfill a great deal of varied responsibilities, they can easily be drawn into a lifestyle that severely drains their energies, leaving them little strength for loving and being loved. For this reason, I advise new brides to resist the temptation of being all things at all times for their man. Even if you are going to be a full time homemaker, for your own sake and the sake of your marriage, gently insist that your love be involved in the various aspects of home-life maintenance. Inform him that the simple act of picking up after oneself goes a very long way towards keeping any home tidy.

If you can afford to hire some home maintenance assistance, you should do so without hesitation. If you cannot afford household help right now, be sure to keep this need in your husband's view as something that you may need in the future, especially when you have small children. In the meantime, try to avoid accumulating lots of "things" and gadgets because they will only add to your burden, as all "things" must be cleaned, stored, repaired, and/or maintained.

Take advantage of the sparkle which is characteristic of the early stages of your marriage to impart your standards and ideals, in this regard, to him. I am reminded of the years when I worked as a labor and delivery nurse. All of the nurses were expected to know how to function in the other areas of the maternity unit just in case they were needed to cover for another nurse or for emergencies. Thus, I was cross-trained as a neonatal and postpartum nurse and sometimes rotated through these areas to keep these skills sharpened. To this end, while you may absolutely love doing all of the ironing, cooking, laundry, dusting, etc., you do yourself a tremendous disservice in the long run if you do not seek to "cross-train" your husband. You should see this, not as a source of discord, but rather as an investment in the strength of your marital bond. This is because when we women are forced to stretch ourselves to the point of physical, spiritual and emotional exhaustion, we lose the ability to nurture ourselves as well as our husbands. I suspect that many divorces are due to this concern, and that we will continue to see this problem persist until more men start to become more like Muhammed in their desire to become truly liberated.

CLEANING TOOLS
Clean living goes a very long way towards preserving our physical health and it also will add to an over-all sense of well being. When your environment is in good order you and your husband will feel more at peace and it is easier to think and function. While there are myriad products and devices that are marketed to help us to keep our bodies and homes clean, there is no more important cleaning tool than the mind whose intent and focus is upon clean living. Even when we are focused upon keeping our homes and possessions clean, it helps to have solid strategies for reducing the amount of time and energy that you must spend in doing-so. Following, are five basics principles that go a very long way towards helping to maintain a clean home and lifestyle:

1). *Careful Hand Washing.* It is well documented that careful hand washing is the very best method for stemming the spread of germs and disease. The Islamic lifestyle places Muslims at an advantage in preventing the spread of disease because our tradition calls for excellent hygiene. Hand washing, in particular, begins the ablution ritual that precedes the daily Islamic prayers. In addition to washing hands as a part of performing the ablution, one should thoroughly wash hands whenever they are exposed to dirt or contaminants. Hand washing should also be done before and after food preparation, eating, and using the bathroom. Keep in mind that the Prophet Muhammed instituted the practice of daily bathing and diligent grooming among the Muslim community as well. And, while both are fairly common today, this traditional attentiveness to personal body cleanliness was not widely practiced in the Middle Ages until Islamic culture began to spread in the world.

2). *Give everything a home.* Set up your home up with intent. Decide where everything in your home "lives" and make others aware of this designation. Use labeling to make this clear to all family members.

3). *Be motion-minded.* Become more aware of how you are moving about within your space. Be particularly aware of what you do with articles of clothing, papers, books etc. whenever you enter or leave a room. I have become aware of having certain "at-risk" times that are more likely to invite disorder. I try become more conscious of what I am doing with my hands and belongings at these times. One of my high-risk times is when I arrive home after being out all day. Even though I am tired, I try to be conscious of where I place my shoes, coat, purse and other bags or articles. If I don't, my arrival can easily wreak havoc upon a perfectly clean room within a few brief minutes. Another time for potential problems is the time of dressing or undressing, especially if you are in a hurry. Make sure you develop the habit of hanging things up immediately. Also keep sufficient hangers on hand for your normal use. You might also prepare outfits the night before so that you have time to put away any unneeded articles of clothing or accessories.

4). *Bring your vision into close focus.* We often have so much on our minds, covering such a wide range of areas, that we withdraw our focus away from the seemingly small or mundane things. Perhaps we do this in an effort to conserve mental energy. The problem with this is that these small things can easily add up to becoming a big mess. If we try to keep our visual focus "tight" within our home we can maintain an environment of cleanliness and order. Try to create the culture of high awareness within your home. Look around and see what is out of place whenever you enter an area. Pick up wayward items quickly, clean up spills, and keep a list in your journal of those items that need to be repaired. You can also delegate tasks to someone else. However, remember that when you delegate duties you are still responsible for following up to make sure that the job is done. What is important is that you keep your home in focus and don't ignore things.

5). *Take time to reset.* Virtually every activity in life requires both preparation actions and reset actions. I explain "the art of the reset" to my children as: preparing a space or item that has been used so that it can be used again safely and pleasurably by another person or by oneself in the future. To this end, we all know how important it is to clean up the kitchen after preparing a meal or after eating. However, we sometimes neglect to properly reset many other activities that require the same type of attention. We may not accurately calculate the amount of time that is necessary to reset after an activity. Sometimes we habitually move on to another activity while a prior one has not been properly concluded. For example, the reset to taking a shower would include: putting dirty clothing in the hamper, cleaning up the shower, closing up bottles and tubes, discarding trash and packaging from newly opened items, wiping up water spills and hanging up towels and washcloths to dry.

I still find it challenging to accurately estimate reset time when embarking upon some activities. However, this skill has improved with time. If this is difficult for you, trust that you will develop a better sense as to how long it realistically takes to perform any particular task.

INTEND YOUR DAYS

Woman's work of every sort requires a great deal of organization, skill and focus. You also deserve to enjoy regular periods of restful rejuvenation. If you don't make plans for how your day is intended to be spent, it will be easy for your day to be seized upon by everything and everyone. If you leave your days open, you can surely rely upon the fact that something, or someone, will inevitably come along to steer you towards a direction that you may not wish to go. Islamic practice calls for important endeavors to be preceded by the act of stating one's intentions. In this same spirit, it is advisable that you write intended plans on paper every day. Note those things that need to get accomplished with top priority and do them first. Even if you intend to relax all day and do absolutely nothing, this should be your intended plan for that day. You will find that if you have children this tool will become vital for survival.

SOME MELANCHOLY

At some time after your wedding day, you may feel a wave of sadness, emptiness, or something indescribable and grey-colored dipping into your mood as you realize that, as a married woman, your life is changed forever. You may suddenly miss your parents or siblings or your small, safe bedroom at home. You may have realized that your husband is not perfect, or that he has discovered that you are not perfect, and that the magic that you thought would be in your heart for him forever has faded just a tiny bit. Some new brides report having a feeling of "who is this man sleeping in my bed?" Tears may flow for no apparent reason, and you may feel that you are isolated and alone.

Try to remember that your life has transitioned immensely from the time that you first decided to marry.

Just as your marriage has been birthed as a new living entity, you may feel that some small part of you has died or been left behind. A very subtle depression or sadness may nip at you. You may also feel guilty or ashamed for having these feelings. However, you should know that this is not abnormal and your feelings are really fine. You may need to visit home, call one of your siblings, or perhaps spend some time with one of your sister-friends for a lunch date. As with any change, marriage is a stress-laden event.

It is well known that happy and pleasant events, or any major changes in your life for that matter, are likely to cause some degree of psychological and physical stress. We think of stress as being caused by negative events; yet, any major change, despite being a very positive one and a source of happiness, can cause a great deal of stress on the body. Though this pressure is not bad, whenever we utilize high amounts of energy, be it physical or emotional, we risk depleting valuable stores of nutrients, thus making it just a bit harder to adjust. For this reason, it is very important to maintain good spiritual and nutritional habits before and after your wedding day. You should be sure to exercise and take your vitamins and any other food supplements that provide you with support.

Pray for a healthy adjustment to your new life and expose yourself to nature in some way each and every day if possible, as the healing energies of the natural world are the most restorative for the human spirit. Most importantly, restore your focus with respect to what your life is supposed to gift to the earth, and do something every day towards that end.

WONDER
Nature is your link to reality, so stay aware and connected to the natural world. When we are disconnected from nature, we are more susceptible to those diseases that can take hold of the spirit and body when one's life is not firmly grounded. If you live in a large city where buildings

and landscapes disrupt successful commune with nature, you should be sure to offer prayers for protection from being pulled into the false world of concrete and grey. You should also take time to look up at the sky often. Even the tall buildings cannot crowd out the sacred sojourn of the blessed clouds. Breathe deeply as you ponder the miraculous cycles that recast this spiritual canvas each day as it also brings essential water to our world, as well as immense beauty to our skies. Seek to learn about the galactic systems of the universe. Look at beautiful photos that depict the different climates, flowers, herbage, and animal life. If you are far away from any signs of nature, grow plants and flowers somewhere in your home, or buy flowers often if you can afford them. Get lots of nature photo-books or posters and purchase audio CD's with recordings of natural healing sounds. Peruse travel photo books so your spirit can recall what it once knew. At night seek out the stars and the moon. Sit still and feel the obedience of your heart as it pumps your spirit throughout your body.

And if you ever feel threatened with being seduced away from trusting in the perfect love of G-d, recall the tender lives of newborn babies. Look upon their faces of every color and kind, and be reunited with the perfect compassion and love of our beautiful Creator. Trust firmly that He will never break His bond with you.

VALUES

Integrity, honesty, accountability and trustworthiness will all likely be tested at some time in your marriage. These ideals are extensions of sacred space that belongs to G-d alone. Being of the same religious faith does not guarantee, by any means, that you and your husband share identical values. Individual Muslims, as well as Muslim communities, vary in their interpretations of scripture and as to what constitutes the most valid ideals of our Prophet Muhammed. Sometimes couples are thus challenged when one has the values of total and complete honesty, while the other believes that degrees of honesty are acceptable while living under a political system that they consider to be predatory. Some may feel that cheating an individual is wrong but perfectly acceptable when one is cheating the government or some city agency.

These situations illustrate the great importance of engaging in careful discussions about real life situations before marriage. It can be very difficult indeed for a wife to stand her ground as to these Islamic values while her love views them somewhat differently. The Quran clearly states that we should preserve justice, whether we are to go against rich or poor or parents or our own selves. It seems that this message invites humanity to the highest standards of integrity. As you are deciding how to handle these challenges, remember that women are the moral compasses that provide strength to the fabric of the entire society. Furthermore, keep in mind that excellent values are essential if we are ever to arrive at peace and a truly civilized existence, and that the principles you uphold will be preserved and passed on to your children and posterity.

CULTURE

Women are, and have always been, the primary guardians of culture. This is a gift as well as a great responsibility because the most valuable human lessons are preserved through culture. Our songs, quilts, recipes, festivals, and crafts all reveal stories as to how people have lived and learned and survived. Women are uniquely gifted with the eye for assessing quickly that which is essentially important and we possess the senses to perceive the best means for collecting life's great lessons and preserving them for our families. Please know that you are serving humanity with the traditions that you initiate and carry on, and thus, with the things that you create and preserve. With this, you protect those invisible stories that are truly important for our survival as a human family; stories of goodness, respect, togetherness, courage, diligence and gratitude. Go forth in the preservation of beautiful humanity as you discover new ways of blending and baking the universal truths into hearty breads, vibrant quilts, vivid songs and all sorts of new recipes for love.

THE BUSINESS OF MARRIAGE

Before I was wed, I spent precious-little time preparing myself for the business of marriage. Love and compatibility issues usually took front and center, while the nuts and bolts of the daily workings of our union were largely relegated to a learn-by-doing process. While in many areas learning by doing is certainly most useful, there are certain discussions and decisions that should be carried out and established from the very outset of your union. Of course, legal documentation that records marriages should be filed. Additionally, bank accounts should be established along with clear mechanisms for paying bills and creating savings. You will also want to establish any other accounts that the both of you deem to be important. Recently, a friend advised me that a background check would not be a bad idea also; couples should fully disclose their credit profile so that there are no surprises later on.

Think about establishing some independent retirement plan for the wife if she chooses to be a stay-at-home mom or for both the wife and the husband, if necessary. Medical and dental insurance should be secured and care also should be taken to ensure that property is recorded properly. Furthermore, it is a good idea to identify a competent family attorney, ideally a Muslim, but at least someone who is familiar with Islamic values. Equally important would be to obtain a consultation with an accountant to determine how your marriage will affect changes in income tax filing for both of you. A financial planner might also be consulted so you can discuss strategies for planning future growth and avoiding common financial traps and errors.

DIFFICULT MATTERS

It is very important to create a few documents and mechanisms to cover those important matters that we often do not like to think about. All adult Muslims should create a Last Will and Testament that clearly states that they are Muslims and that they request a simple Islamic burial. This is especially important in the United States and Canada or other countries where extended family members may not be aware of these traditions. Sometimes families are unwilling to bury a Muslim family member Islamically, simply because they are unclear as to the proper Islamic funeral rites. The Will document should also give instructions as to how property and inheritance shall be dispersed, again deferring to the Islamic codes.

Couples should also designate Advance Medical Directives, also known as a "Living Will." This document gives clear legal authority for making medical decisions for someone who is incapable of making these themselves due to some form of incapacitation. It is my strong opinion that this authority should remain with parents. However, in some cases some joint authority might be arrived at requiring agreement between parents and the spouse. Legal guardians should be declared for surviving children. Couples should also discuss Eldercare concerns with their spouses. It is important that both husband and wife request that their own parents also create necessary documents to cover these types of issues. This is because it is very likely at some point that you both will be actively involved in assisting your parents with these matters in the future.

HEALTH

Making a commitment to good health is the most valid investment that you both can make towards your healthy future as a couple. Muslims have been instructed by Muhammed that "the body has rights over you." We are further informed that, on the Day of Judgment, the body will testify as to how well we cared for it while it was in our charge. Hopefully, healthy habits are already a part of your and your husband's premarital lifestyle. Even if this is not the case, there is always so much that can be done to improve health habits and to initiate a healthier lifestyle.

Firstly, prior to affirming the marriage agreement, both bride and groom should obtain a comprehensive physical examination and undergo tests to ensure that neither has been exposed to any disease that may be communicable to their new spouse. Couples should also make a commitment to eating a variety of fresh healthy foods, while remembering that the consumption of wholesome foods is enjoined upon Muslims by G-d in the Quran. Muhammed's traditions are rich with healthy eating advisements; perhaps one of the best ones is that we should stop eating before our stomachs have become filled. Also, remember that it is highly recommended that all women take a folic acid B vitamin supplement for at least a year prior to becoming pregnant to help to prevent birth defects.

Keep in mind that poor physical health can be the indirect cause of a myriad of marital problems such as: irritability, cloudy judgment, and compromised self-esteem. Sometimes, when couples find that they are not relating well with one another, the cause can be traced to health concerns which are subtly interfering with good, clean communication.

MARRIAGE
Marriage will likely provide the best earthly opportunity for you to manifest your best self as a human being. Marriage inspires you to confront your ability to fulfill your best dreams of who you can become, while forcing your wounds, fears and insecurities to the surface. The stresses and challenges of marriage act to purge and purify us as we also gratify and satiate our deepest, truest selves. Marriage stirs alive an awareness that allows us to be complete,

whole individuals, while also being recognized as individual parts of the whole of humanity. We become more aware of having been selected for the highest honors as servants of The Inventor of our Earth and the heavens. In marriage, we are re-birthed again and again, as we are connected somehow to all that has been and is yet still to come.

THIS NEW BABY

I have advised many couples to regard their new marriage as if it were a newborn baby. In their new marriage, they are possessed of a delicate new life that should be cherished, nourished, responded to, and protected from all harm. I love this metaphor because it really brings to life the idea that marriage requires serious effort, yet its precious life is full of marvelous potential. I try to remind couples that one wouldn't even think of discarding an infant child when it cries or poops or even falls down as she attempts to learn to walk or run. This would, of course, be absurd. Like newborn infants, new marriages should be swaddled and held close to the breast and fed continuously around the clock, day and night, on demand. We should also take great care to cleanse away impurities as quickly as possible so that soreness and wounds do not ensue as a result of the break down in the integrity of delicate new skin.

When our toddlers, fascinated with the word "no," begin to flaunt their newfound power, we wait patiently for this brief phase of egocentricity to pass on. And we continue to show off our new baby with joy and pride to all who will look upon her—as we also relish the glint of a smile that is so very similar to your mother's, to his uncle's, or to ancestors forgotten or unknown. As this precious child matures, there are, of course, new hurdles to overcome as she pursues her desire to touch the eternal life-line, yet we do finally arrive at a time when this precious child is beautiful, whole, and independent. Thus, your marriage becomes a marvelous reflection of G-d's mercy and also a reflection of your faith in G-d's excellent plan.

WORRY

The tendency to worry seems to be pervasive within our culture and indeed within human nature. We worry about loss of love, money, or our reputations. We worry about sickness, loneliness, and death. It may be that we sometimes believe that if we are duly devoted to adequate time spent worrying, we are actually changing our circumstances or preventing a feared event from occurring. I wish that I myself knew how to worry less and trust in G-d and in my own abilities more, because worry doesn't seem to change anything. This emotion only takes up precious space within the psyche. I have heard it said that worry is a manifestation of a misdirected imagination! This idea suggests that we are capable of using the same mental energy that we use for worrying to focus on and imagine positive solutions and successful outcomes, rather than to allow our spirits to be enveloped by spasms of fear and panic.

When you are threatened by worries, try writing down what you are actually afraid of. Take those fears to G-d continuously and listen for the response when the Supreme Voice of Goodness, Love, and Healing responds. This does wonders! It is also beneficial to recall that G-d promises that He listens to the call of every suppliant; therefore, we should listen to His call in a state of willingness to *do* something different. If you are capable of changing something, even if it involves some risk or some fear, consult with your husband-partner, and then do it! Don't wait for your problems to disappear. Make them do so, with G-d's help.

You might also try giving yourself pep talks to help you to get through the most frightening parts of your sojourn. Give yourself the same type of encouraging advice that you would give to your dearest friend if she had become overwhelmed by her fears. Do whatever it takes to change your circumstances so that worry doesn't claim your health, which it is most certainly capable of doing! Know that in every endeavor that you, as a G-d conscious person, undertake towards doing any good thing, The Ever-Merciful G-d is sustaining, protecting and aiding you. Just continue to have courage and believe wholeheartedly in Him.

STRESS, EFFICIENCY AND JIHAD

It is said that the Prophet Muhammed advised that we should avoid doing things in the extreme because anything done in the extreme cannot be maintained for long. With this in mind, try not to subject yourself to undue stress if you can at all help it. This principle invites us to be efficient in our use of energy and to avoid creating unnecessary stress as a demonstration of some sort of ability to endure superhuman sacrifices. We are told that if Muhammed knew of two ways to perform any task, he always selected the method that was easiest or most efficient. This is to say that there is no need to put oneself into stressful circumstances unnecessarily.

Make life as comfortable for yourself as you possibly can so that you can be a source of comfort and relief for your family. Maintain a peaceful countenance and avoid placing yourself into stressful situations unless this is truly necessary for the protection of your family or community. Conserve your energies for those inevitable periods in life when you will be forced to exert yourself for good reasons.

As women, there will always be times when we must focus spiritual energy towards achieving some important goal or major achievement. This concept is known to Muslims as *Jihad*. We are exhorted by G-d to struggle and exert ourselves in this way throughout our lives, and the fruits of these struggles will soon come into view. Muslims are especially encouraged to struggle for the goal of self-improvement, as Muhammed advised that *Jihad-ul*

Nafs—the internal struggle to gain control over the self/soul—is the greatest *Jihad.*

OF BUSINESS AND PLEASURE
When marriage is exposed to physical violence or emotional cruelty there can be no business or pleasure. Couples simply cannot build trusting relationships in an atmosphere of fear and pain. However, I am not of the opinion that wives, or husbands for that matter, need muddy the business of having simple disagreements by withholding physical comfort from one another. It seems to me that one should take full advantage of whatever glue brings you together, while allowing the natural forces that G-d has placed within the atmosphere to reconfigure and re-magnetize the very nature of your thoughts and minds and perhaps even the disagreement itself.

YOUR HAIR
When your hair is not healthy and well-styled, you will most likely not be truly happy–at least not deep down inside yourself. As superficial as this may seem, I have noted within my own life that there is a direct correlation between my mood and the condition of my hair. Poorly groomed hair communicates to your husband the level of care that you are expecting from him as well. As an investment in your peace of mind as well in as your marriage, always try to maintain a healthy and beautiful head of hair.

COOKING
I absolutely love to cook, yet, I don't like to do it all the time. If your husband cooks, you are blessed indeed! If he doesn't know how to cook, it would be nice to bring him into the kitchen with you in the early part of your marriage. Even if he only cooks a tiny bit, no matter what he cooks for you, tell him that it is superb, and mean it! When you are nursing a new baby at three o'clock in the morning

even a tuna fish sandwich will taste like swordfish steak! I feel strongly that all men, women and older children should know their way around the basics of the kitchen. However, if you are presently the only reliable cook in your home, you should take some breaks from cooking to keep your interests alive. Can you imagine doing any job incessantly for one or even two years without a small vacation of some sort?

Plan meals and shopping skillfully, and be sure to eat leftovers or sandwiches on grocery shopping days. Learn to batch cook to ease up time. In this way, you can store up meals so that you are able to take some time off from cooking as the family eats the foods that have been laid away in preparation for your "cooking vacation." Try new recipes to make cooking more interesting and more adventurous. If neither of you know how to cook, you should set out to learn together by practicing recipes with each other. Try to make these times fun and romantic.

YOUR METTLE

Sadly, life does deliver bad moments, sad moments and very hard days. When faced with such days, my husband reminds me that G-d tells us in the Quran that He will test us as to our "reported mettle." We are also questioned as to whether we are under the impression that we will enter the paradise without being tested. The Quran further instructs us that during times of difficulty we are to "Call on G-d, much and often." This suggests that we improve our remembrance of G-d in quality as well as in quantity. Thus, we are to work on trusting in G-d more fully by bringing His name to the forefront of our psyche regularly.

In this regard, we are never to be ashamed of needing the help of G-d or of calling on G-d with longing when you are afraid or troubled. Remember that G-d is your only true friend. If you are ashamed to call on G-d, make no mistake that you are soundly in the grips of *Shaytan*— the presence that invites human beings to be despondent, to lose trust in G-d, or to think that we should have somehow been already perfected like angels and should be ashamed of being human. Also, know that when we are tempted to walk down the road of distrust, haughtiness or despair, we can rebound instantaneously—for G-d states that the *Shaytan* has no power over man except that which man relinquishes to him. Like our first father, Adam, we as humans are endowed with special gifts which are best revealed only after we have struggled, faltered, repented and conquered.

DINNERTIME

Set a dinner time and stick to it, please. This habit will serve you for years to come. This will help you maintain a schedule and it will ingrain a valuable tradition that is proven to give families an edge against the influences and pressures of the outside world. Buy a few small items that make dinnertime special. Table settings, candles, and good napkins are all items that can be purchased or made very inexpensively. If you were given these gifts for your wedding, use them! The arrival of children may threaten to make these special dinners less likely, but you will find that children absolutely love the security of the ritual of dinnertime.

RESTORE

Please take some time to restore yourself daily. I myself am still learning to practice this lesson. Rest your body with short naps throughout the day. Even a five or ten minute nap can help you to recharge. Restore your spirit through prayer, meditation, and quiet reflection. Restore your confidence by guarding against the voices that inspire doubt or despair.

ADMIRE

Your admiration is food and drink for your love's spirit. If you admire him or something that he has done, said, or intended to do, tell him and show him how much you appreciate his actions. How often have I witnessed the most charitable of wives warming toward any stranger's request, while leaving their love's spirit languishing in the hot desert sun, as he longs for even a tiny sip of water from her kind lips.

ADMISSIONS AND APOLOGIES
If you have erred, admit that you have done so and make amends. Your sincere demonstration educates him as to the superb and superior qualities of the resilience of the repentant soul.

MY WOMEN
You will likely find that the strongest influences upon your values as a woman, wife, and mother, have primarily been imparted by your own mother as well as other women in your family. I personally can see aspects of all the women in my family within my own personality. It can be very helpful to isolate these feminine presences within your psychological sphere so as to be more aware of how each one has impacted your life. Most of these influences are likely very positive, but you may also find, in some cases, you will have to take care not to imitate aspects of those personalities which do not correspond with your life or values.

My earliest memories of my mother recall her as being a beautiful, bright, young student. She was hardworking and focused, but also bitter and angry much of the time due to hardships she'd experienced during her marriage to my father. My father apparently suffered from severe post-traumatic stress disorder as a result of his military service in World War II, during which he served in Europe, as well as the South Pacific. My mother's persistent mantra was that of "survival." Meanwhile, she constantly taught us about African-American history and the African-American freedom movement. We were always exposed to loads of books and records that gave insight into the struggles of African-American people and we were also given some exposure to the teachings of the so-called "Black Muslims."

My mother was very health conscious. She always promoted healthy eating, as well as taking nutritional supplements and vitamins. She forbade television because, as an educator, she insisted that the effects of T.V. were extremely damaging to children. My mother was also a very good financial manager and strongly disciplined insofar as not buying excessive material things. She always lived frugally, preferring instead to invest and save for the future.

My mother's influence sparks ideals such as independence, self-reliance, liberation and love. However, she also imparted the message that men could not really be trusted. I knew better than to embrace this message, having been raised by a very responsible and trustworthy grandfather, yet my mother's fears have plagued me at critical times during my marriage.

While I value my mother's exemplary character in a great many areas, I most value the spiritual values that she imparted to me. She studied the spiritual principles of Buddhism, Christian Science, and Silent Unity. However, my mother informed my brothers and me that she preferred we choose our own religion when we were old enough to make a good decision. The only requirement she insisted upon was that we not worship a human being as G-d. When I became exposed to *Al-Islam*, I was very much attracted to the Quran's message because of its consistency with my mother's early advisement. For this reason, while my mother remains a practitioner of Christian Science, I am forever indebted to her for helping me to choose *Al-Islam* for my religion. I also credit my mother for inspiring me with a strong appetite for understanding religious principles. More than anything, I am grateful that she afforded me my intellectual and religious freedom.

My maternal grandmother, Flora, was also very intelligent and very focused on the ideal of continuously gaining an education. However, my grandmother's strongest character trait was that she worked extremely hard. In fact, Grandma Flora's work ethic was absolutely dizzying! She worked incessantly at her job and went to college at night, while also taking care of housework, yard-work, and gardening. My grandmother insisted upon helping my mother to raise my brothers and me. Therefore, she was also an "acting" mother for her grandchildren.

Grandma Flora even petitioned to be allowed to work beyond the retirement age of sixty-five, which she successfully accomplished by working until she was well into her seventies. She and my grandfather were a team, but they were constantly fussing. I am sure that this is why I tend to be fussy with my husband when I become stressed. I also learned from Grandma Flora that women were to work constantly, taking little or no time for themselves. My grandmother insisted upon doing all of the housework because she felt that no one could do it as thoroughly as she could. This was unfortunate for me because, as a new bride, I was unaccustomed to doing serious housework. In fact, my husband had to teach me how to perform housecleaning and laundry duties proficiently. However, I did inherit Grandma Flora's tendency for being in constant motion: working myself to exhaustion most of the time, feeling terribly guilty if I took any time for myself. While I love my grandmother more than words can ever say, Grandma Flora's example has also taught me that women must learn when, and how, to relax. We should try to step back and allow others— especially our children—to learn, grow and make their own competent contribution to the maintenance and function of the household.

My maternal great-grandmother "Granny" was a practical nurse. Granny was an excellent cook and an exceedingly proficient homemaker. Her home was always decorated stylishly and kept meticulously clean. Even her pots and pans were kept perfectly polished at all times. Granny upheld the traditional values of being a gracious southern lady, as well as those of being a good Christian woman. I spent more time with Granny than I spent with anyone else while growing up. I came upstairs to her apartment after school every day to assist her with the cooking and light cleaning while chatting with her about life and the little lessons that she thought were important. On Sundays, I accompanied Granny to her church, where she was a member for sixty years. Granny taught me how to set a table and how to eat with proper table etiquette. In preparation for holidays, I was charged with wrapping presents, addressing cards, and polishing her silver. I enjoyed all of this immensely.

I especially enjoyed being in Granny's home because this is where all of our other family members would inevitably congregate. My Aunt Mamie and her daughter, Mildred, were always stopping by. Aunt Mamie was very petite and very striking, as she had an interesting mixture of African-American and Native-American facial features. I also remember being fascinated with Aunt Mamie's magnificent collection of refurbished "orphaned" dolls. My favorite cousin, Sharon, would also come to stay with Granny for the entire summer. Granny's home was a special place of refuge for me. I realize that as an adult, I am always subconsciously trying to re-create the same atmosphere in my home that I enjoyed while growing up in hers. Yet, I must sometimes force myself to be less demanding as I realize that, unlike mine, Granny's home had not been continuously stressed by the presence of so many busy and active children.

At times, my other great-grandmother, Mary, also lived with us. Living to be one hundred and four years old, she was feisty, agile and very athletic well into her eighties. Grandma Mary loved G-d tremendously. Although she was Christian, she worshipped wholeheartedly among any congregation or denomination that invited her in, whether they were Christian, Jewish, or Muslim. Grandma Mary instructed all of us grandchildren at an early age that, "Although we may call Him by different names, there is only One G-d!" She said this with such forcefulness that I sensed this was the one idea, above all others, that she truly believed in.

Despite her age, Grandma Mary could be very provocative. Even at the age of one hundred, she relished playfully making brides and married ladies alike, blush by telling them about all of the fun they should be having with their husbands!

My paternal grandmother Hazel, whom we affectionately called "Grandma-Mom," also lived to see the one hundred years mark. She was a master dressmaker/seamstress and she also decorated birthday and wedding cakes. I was stunned upon first seeing one of these lavish, gorgeous cakes and wondered why she never chose to decorate cakes professionally. Grandma-Mom also served as an officer for the International Ladies Garment Worker's Union. She exuded an aura of regality and as a young girl; I was always tremendously intimidated by her because she seemed so perfectly cultured. Grandma-Mom was also famously punctual and would query any one who was even two minutes delayed for an appointment, as to why they were so late!

Grandma-Mom was very well-read and very articulate, despite not having been college educated. She was also extremely fashionable. I have never encountered my grandmother not stylishly dressed and meticulously bejeweled, wearing her baubles, bangles, and high-heels all the way up to the week before she passed away. I am always inspired by Grandma-Mom's example insofar as taking care of myself. Her example continues to inspire me to promote fashion and beauty among other women.

Aunt Mildred was actually my cousin but I was instructed to call her "aunt" because she was some thirty years older than me. Mildred always dressed beautifully and her hair was always styled in the most current hairstyles. She had a sweet, agreeable demeanor and a quick sense of humor, but, she could also flash a no-nonsense look that made you know to take her seriously. As a child, I especially loved Mildred because she was the first person to ever take me to a shopping mall! Most importantly, Mildred exemplified the best qualities of being a wife and mother and she served as a terrific role model for me as a married woman.

Mildred had married her husband while he was an active serviceman during World War II. While he was away, Mildred dutifully squirreled away all of the military paychecks that my uncle sent her. When my uncle returned home, he found that she had saved enough money to make a nice down payment on their first home!

I always noticed that Mildred spoke about my uncle with girlish fondness and sincere admiration, even when she was not in his presence. It was so easy to tell that she respected and loved her husband, as she always guarded his reputation in just the same way that she'd guarded the money that he'd sent her during the War. Mildred had difficulty conceiving a baby for nine years and considered herself exceedingly blessed when she finally became pregnant with her first and only child. Despite this difficulty, she was like a second mother to many other children within her community.

It was quite touching to see Mildred and my uncle in her later years after she'd become seriously physically debilitated. My uncle took care of her with great tenderness, devotion, and diligence for some eleven years until she passed away. They were abundantly blessed to have enjoyed a wonderful marriage that was filled with love, devotion, and tranquility for sixty-three years.

My great-aunt, Estella, is also a very, very special lady whose life has served to inspire all of the women in my family. Having been a domestic worker most of her life, she virtually raised many of her employers' children. She has a very wise way with young people and she always seems to know just what to say to inspire them. Aunt Estella continuously advises that parents avoid yelling at their children and, instead, learn to teach them with consistency, love, and discipline.

At the ripe age of ninety-two years, my aunt Estella is still quite strong. She cherishes her independence greatly and very rarely allows anyone to assist her in getting out and about. She insists that she needs to stay busy in order to get her exercise. Aunt Estella always says that she doesn't like to complain about, or focus upon, being sick: even if she is under the weather, she prefers to say that she feels great! Aunt Estella says that she has seen many women talk themselves into serious illnesses by continuously complaining, rather than practicing living a life of gratitude. And Aunt Estella has never even heard about "The Secret!" (of quantum theory, as it relates to the power of our human thoughts upon our lives). However, she readily credits her wisdom to G-d's guidance as given in the proverbial biblical advisement: "As a man thinketh in his heart, so is he."

WOMEN IN WHITE

As I approached my teenage years, life seemed to become a bit foggy...hazy. American values were changing rapidly in the 1970's and I was starting to think that the wholesome and decent principles that my Granny had imparted to me were from a different world or that I was going crazy. That was until I met those elegant women in white. The image of the Muslim women from the so-called Black Muslim movement was so powerful in my spirit and in my mind. They represented my silent hope that goodness, innocence, refinement and beauty were alive and well somewhere, although America's ever-changing culture now seemed to reflect otherwise. In these women, I saw the best of the women in my family and my neighborhood. These sisters somehow managed to hold on to the simple decency of womanhood that I'd cherished seeing in my community when I was growing up. Muslim women represented cleanliness, compassion and a willingness to make sacrifices in order to preserve the sacred values of our community. Muslim women exemplified dedication to motherhood and family life and they supported the good works that good men were doing within our neighborhoods. These women were serious about protecting the lives of their children. They sought to protect them by providing the community with private school education so as to prevent youngsters from soaking up negativity and despair.

Later on, I met many more Muslim women from other communities and from other parts of the world. Again, I witnessed the sense of seriousness for preserving the good life of G-d consciousness, and serving our fellow man. I was appreciated and encouraged by all of these lovely women and they wasted no time in attempting to teach me how to live my life cleanly and conscientiously. I was educated, disciplined and loved by them. And when I suffered any disappointment, they held me. I wish the world could know how magnificent it was to be in the company of those wonderful women in white and I will always remember their great legacy.

THE THEATRE
Marriage sometimes has the interesting tendency to heave up all sorts of stuff from our past, sparking the most vivid reenactments of the most sensitive psychological episodes

in our lives. For some reason, marriage often seems to create the perfect set up for a kind of psycho-emotional theatre. Thus, when we are feeling rejected we are called back to the times in our childhood when we were left out. When we are feeling happy in our marriage, we are carried back to the happiest days of play or security when we were young children at home. When we are angry, we become the little girl who is feeling outraged that she has been sent to her room. This theatre can also dredge up the hurts of trauma or abuse.

It is believed that biochemical similarities between past and current emotional states can be the cause of these emotional patterns. We may find that our husband's words or gestures might sometimes cause us to feel threatened as if we are to be traumatized once again, as we might have been in the past, perhaps when we were young and vulnerable. This can occur with men as well as women. Although it can be very challenging, try to separate from these cycles before they begin. If the problems are severe and persistent, you might also seek out professional counseling assistance. Strive to arrive at an emotional place that shifts this paradigm instantaneously, as if in mid air. If and when the curtain goes up, threatening to reprise past performances of tragic dramas, simply take a final bow and then leap off of this stage of past psychological traumas. Run courageously out of that old, dilapidated theatre; down the aisle towards the beautiful new lives that you and your new love have so much hope and promise for building together.

THE "D" WORD
Before I got married, a friend of mine who had recently ended her marriage said to me that she regretted the day she first brought up the word "divorce." She told me that once this word had surfaced and been spoken aloud, it seemed to consume their marriage. Every time a challenge presented itself, this word, having been given a seat,

festered like a parasite upon the very life-blood of their marriage. My friend instructed me never to even mention the "D" word in my marriage.

I wish that I could say that I had listened to her advice. Sadly, I must admit that I also sometimes invited this word in, giving it space that it did not deserve. Sophisticated justifications such as "incompatibility" make the "D" word seem a reasonable one, as if this path might offer up some real solution for solving the challenges of marriage. The "D" word's presence is often seated deceptively just over in the corner, pretending to be innocent, as if it were simply a butterfly or sprout of hyssop when in fact it is a cruel fire breathing dragon! In most cases, the presence and mention of the "D" word only complicates matters. The careless use of this word will only take up the valuable time and space, both of which, you and your love will need precious amounts of, in order to master the work of parenting your new relationship towards making it one that is the source of abundance and restful serenity.

RECEIVING

The woman, unable to warmly receive her love's love, has thereby ultimately failed at love's giving.

WORDS

The power of your words for doing enormous good or harm can never, ever be underestimated. An exceedingly wise Islamic scholar once said that "words make people, and people are a product of words." Your marriage is birthed through the words of your vows and the agreements of your contract, yet is nourished properly through its infancy by the milk-filled words of trust and love, and simplistic words like the "oohs" and "aahs" that reflect the joy of sincere giving and receiving.

Of course, at times you will have to use words to inform and describe feelings of hurt, confusion, and disappointment. Still, do not allow your tongue to become a trajectory for the launching of those words better suited to be used against a drug peddler or a convicted inside trader, rather than an erring husband.

Yes, in marriage you will occasionally have to express outrage, anger, or sadness. You will, and indeed you must do so, if you desire to feed the delicate new life of your marriage upon the pristine foundation of honesty and truth. Yet, you will likely find out that you can accurately correct most issues by focusing upon how certain actions make you feel, or the effect that they had upon a situation, rather than on defining actions as proof of negative character judgments about him.

COMMUNICATION

If I were you I wouldn't waste much time making too many solemn pronouncements as to the need for the two of you to experience better communication—especially while having the hope that your verbal observation will somehow solve a specific communication concern. For some reason, whenever I mention the word "communication," my love and I seem to instantaneously lose some of our ability to communicate effectively. I don't know why this is so, yet it is often true. Perhaps it is like demanding that our children eat healthy foods and take their vitamins, rather than simply preparing a tasty, healthy meal and serving it to them.

Rather than talking too much about "communication," focus on accurately describing the concerns that are on your mind and try to listen carefully for solutions which might help you to resolve the issues at hand.

CRITICISM

I truly don't like my husband to criticize me. I really don't like it at all. He does so rarely, I think, because he knows how sensitive I am. It's not because I am unaware of having faults; it's just that the criticism doesn't seem to take into consideration the ever-present extenuating circumstances that I am always seemingly facing. It is only recently that I am beginning to understand that his criticisms can be heard without my feeling the need to take them so personally. In this regard, I hope you ladies are much better than I.

MOODS

I don't think that I was aware for the first fifteen years of marriage that I experienced periodic monthly cyclical changes in mood. When I finally realized that these powerful sensations of frustration could be clocked by the moon, I really felt so much better. I was relieved in knowing that it was possible that my intense feelings might be just a bit exaggerated due to powerful underlying biochemical events. I felt humbled in the awareness that my body was in concert with the same rhythms that hold the Earth in its orbit and cause the rising of the tides.

I now also know that my husband's moods can be altered by his own biological rhythms, as well as hunger, a lack of sleep, or challenging concerns at work. When I am aware of the presence of any one of these factors, I try to overlook small matters while still withdrawing into some degree of silence, so as to make him aware that something that he has said or done has registered. I do this, not because I am angry, but rather because I don't like "the General" to forget that this foot soldier is still a sensitive woman.

PAIN

The Quran states that human beings are created in pain and struggle. This, I believe, encourages us to value immensely the human life we have suffered so much to give birth to. The *fear* of pain, however, can stifle life's progress in many hidden ways. We also know that one of the strongest motivations for human achievement is the avoidance of pain.

During childbirth, when we mothers first experience strong labor pains, we are shocked and shaken. Laboring women very often tense up in anticipation of the next wave of pain and then the tense muscle response creates a further heightened sensation of pain. Thus, the fear of pain creates more pain than the actual uterine contraction causes itself. When we know what to expect from pain, we are more capable of managing our focus to handle it. So, when the first inevitable challenge to the security of your love-bond washes over your relationship, you can either strive to take some deep breaths, trusting that G-d's plan is delivering your marriage towards harmony and excellence, or you can allow fear of the not-so-inevitable to overcome all of your senses.

It is rare indeed that marriages do not deliver some form of pain, humiliation, or hurt. Trust that the pain will eventually subside and that you will swaddle, cuddle and embrace your love anew.

CURVES
Didn't you just love it when your teacher took into account the small details of inequity during a particularly grueling semester? Even now, I can hear the rumors whispered up and down the hallway. "Did you hear that the final exam will be graded on a curve? Now I might still make the honor roll." I always beg my love to grade my efforts on a curve trusting that my intentions are the best, though the house may not always be perfectly clean and the children not always in perfect order. If your husband is a general, unaccustomed to cutting the troops some slack, you might offer up some small token or gift that speaks to his softer side.

CLUTTER
Try to avoid the cluttering of your home at all costs. This can be difficult because of our propensity for possessing those "things" which have become so important to the

daily living of modern life. I have found clutter to operate subversively, undoing the peace that is native to my spirit. Whenever some space is uncluttered or re-ordered, I am liberated in ways in which I had not realized I'd been oppressed. This event has occurred often enough in my life for me to know that clutter is actually a form of psychological oppression! Remember that personal and community cleanliness is one of the most vital and significant characteristics—and historical distinctions—of Islamic life and culture. Please commit to creating a home for every single object in your abode, down to the toothpicks and the screw of unknown origin. This is not to say that every item will be in its place at all times, but when time permits, the orphaned item can at least be restored to its proper home.

HIS FRIENDS

One of the greatest challenges for many new brides is in understanding a husband's strong need to socialize with his friends. While some men are content to spend most of their spare time with their new bride, others have a very strong need to maintain strong bonds with male friends. I have come to believe that the strong need that many males exhibit for bonding in groups is an evolutionary advantage for human beings. Men have historically been responsible for defending their groups and tribes from violence. Thus, the male tendency to cultivate strong camaraderie with other males is a sort of preparation for the ever-present possibility of having to secure their families. Men have needed to belong to a capable and reliable group of men who would be loyal against any threats and in the heat of battle.

In modern times, men continue to gather in these groups as if practicing for their battles through sparring with one another verbally. They prepare for warfare vicariously via the pseudo-wars of sports games, or talk about the strengths and weaknesses of other men, thus employing some measure of strategic planning as if participating in a war council. Now, there certainly can be big problems if the friends your man has chosen for his army are single or not particularly supportive of marriage. However, in some ways these single men might be considered as being great council members because they are not as obligated as their married counterparts and thus, theoretically, might be more available for "battle." Notwithstanding this theory, it is likely far more true that their married male friends will inevitably be wiser, more reliable, and better negotiators because they understand much better the value of the family. They also intimately feel the importance of keeping peace in the land for the sake of securing their own wife and children.

Having said all of this, I must admit that I have demonstrated very little tolerance for my husband spending large amounts of time with comrades, especially those who are not yet married. My discomfort with this has sometimes caused almost irreparable rifts between us. I am truly not proud of this, but one day after having a terribly heated argument about his friends, I impulsively called up several of them to complain. One of his friends happened to be a very wise and kind, older gentleman. This man spoke to me with immense warmth and sensitivity, confiding in me the details of the pain of the divorce that he had long ago experienced. He spoke with caring and sincerity and he began tearfully begging me to have patience for my husband while reminding me of my love's excellent human and manly qualities. He said that our marriage was like a very beautiful tall building and that, in my haste and impatience, I might inadvertently cause a beautiful monument to come crumbling down. His words made me think about the Quranic verses that warn that we not be like the woman who carelessly unravels her bundle of yarn, after having worked so hard to spin it tightly. I was amazed and humbled by this wise elder's confidence. Since that day, I have come to better understand that the strong bonds between men can also serve to reinforce their commitment to their wives and children.

MAIL
Be especially cautious of mail. Mail is both friend and foe, bringing good news and helpful notifications, yet also threatening to burden your days with temptations and distractions. Mail can also easily fill your home with pounds of needless, disorganized clutter. On a daily basis you must open and take charge of the handling of your mail. Mail handling should be done at the point of entry to your home. When handling mail be near your calendar—with pen in hand. You should also have your recycling/trash bin nearby. Place bills and mail that involves some future action in their proper receptacles and place your husband's mail in the area that he wishes it to be placed. Junk mail should be immediately trashed— recycled—and mail of importance is to be placed in the properly labeled receptacle. You should have files or receptacles that are labeled with a person's name or an intended action. Furthermore, I do not open my husband's mail unless given permission. The same is true for him.

BEAUTY
I was raised by my grandmother to keep my focus upon education and intellect rather than on my beauty. Thus, when I married I had to learn the cultural values of beauty. I felt myself cast so differently from the beauties in those magazines that I decided that I perhaps, could lay no claim to beauty. When I asked my love if I was beautiful and if he found me pretty despite my not looking like the women in those magazines, he said he'd always thought I was very beautiful, until I started to reveal my insecurities by asking him all of these silly questions.

BEAUTY REGIMEN

Read Scripture trusting the Perfect Love of G-d. Drink plenty of water. Smile at elderly people and at babies, their mothers, and all caretakers. Eat fresh, uncooked fruits and vegetables. Pray with a sincere heart, knowing that G-d is right there, although you cannot see Him. Drink green vegetable juices as often as you can. Try to think and say the best about all people. Exercise and beautify your body every day. Detoxify your mind from despair and self-doubt daily. Begin working towards a goal that excites you and makes you feel alive. Forgive that person who did that horrible thing to you. Take your vitamins and those supplements that help you. Pray for your loved ones and every person that you can think of who needs prayer. Observe the natural world and read about its wonders. Eat good quality food in moderate quantities throughout the day. Ask G-d to forgive you, your family and all of humanity. Smile and share what you have with others. Pray for the efforts of the good leaders in our world. Take walks and stretch. Pray that G-d will bless the poor, as well as the wealthy, and that He will restore our Earth-home into a garden of peace and security.

SECRETS

I do not like to have secrets from my husband. They make me feel disconnected from him, and he truly is my best and dearest friend. Yet, we all have some private aspects of our selves that can never be shared, even if we wanted to. I try to understand that my husband also has a private place that is sensed on my radar but can never be really viewed or captured.

HORMONES

After four children and two husbands, Sister Sherry said that she was just starting to understand the hormonal patterns and cycles of her childbearing body. One day she told me, "You know, I think that I never would have split

96

up with my first husband had I known all of this stuff about myself!"

SERVICE
You will likely feel a void in your marriage and your life until you embrace the fact that your best self is connected to the lives of all others on the Earth. Indeed, embracing the needs of all humanity is the only way for you to have real inner peace. According to our Prophet Muhammed, if we are not free to change something overtly, we can strike the world's consciousness with our voices; if this is not possible, we are at least to pursue our work with the strength of our hearts. Even our facial expressions and silent body language can give others a visible image as to what is ruminating in our hearts. We can also pray continuously for help to be provided for those in need and we should trust and know that the days when goodness prevails over all else will certainly come.

SELECTIVE MEMORY
What is it about anger that causes some lovers to suddenly acquire selective memories? In the throes of anger, I can't recall anything good that my love has done or said. Yet, I can recall with perfect accuracy and alphabetically, every insensitive, selfish or overbearing thing that he has done or said against me. I am furthermore incensed if he dares to bring forth a corresponding listing of any things which I might have inadvertently said or done against him.

HE NOTICES
Do not make the mistake of thinking that, because he is a man, your husband doesn't sense or feel or notice small betrayals of doubt as to his abilities. He is likely very adept at reading your cues of distrust and non-commitment. He may not say that he is very sensitive and that you hurt his feelings when you insulted, teased, or made fun of him... but trust that it registered negatively within his spirit,

especially if it was done in front of his brother, your sister, your mother, or a friend. I have found men to be more outwardly resilient when fielding small seemingly innocent criticisms. However, they are often silently unraveling ties to you and in some minute measure, disconnecting themselves from you. If your comments are not designed to help, just leave them unsaid, for they certainly will not serve to strengthen your marriage tie.

SENSIBILITY
I just love this word! I even like the way it sounds. It is so neat and melodic and precise. Sensibility always suggests to me that I do what makes sense, despite the forces and whims that are tempting to pull me about in several other digressive directions. People say that sensibility is overrated, which suggests that life is not lived fully unless we are living impulsively and spontaneously, throwing all caution to the wind. However, I have found that this characteristic can always be soundly relied upon for guiding oneself through everyday life, as well as through the turbulence and clouds that threaten sound living.

MUSIC LESSONS
What if a great musician's priceless violin, carved with the finest spruce and sycamore, joined with the strongest glues and fitted with the sturdiest of supple strings, then tuned and polished with the finest resins—after having been idealized and yearned upon for months or years or even for what seems to have been a lifetime—when taken into his performance chambers, refuses to release its sweet and spirited songs of joy, despite being played with expertise, passion, grace, sincerity and goodly inspiration?

SLEEPING RHYTHMS
Many couples have difficulties with issues surrounding biorhythms and sleep-wake patterns, so it would be a good idea to find out whether you and your love tend to sleep

and awaken at approximately the same times. If you have different cycles in this area, you'll probably experience some marital challenges because of this. For example, you both may be left feeling disappointed when you discover that your habit of sleeping late on the weekends disrupts his deeply held fantasies about taking brisk Saturday morning power-walks with his new bride! Try to discuss these concerns beforehand so that you can arrive at some happy compromise. Adjustments in this area can certainly be made, but don't underestimate the challenge.

DAYS OF DISPLEASURE

Please trust me when I tell you that there may be a few moments, or even days, when you really, really, don't like the man who is now calling himself your husband! His flaws are magnified because of something done or said that was void of sensitivity, intelligence or accuracy. These are moments to turn to G-d in earnest prayer. It is likely that it will not be too long before something occurs that informs you with precision and clarity, once again, as to why you are blessed immensely and profoundly in being mated with him.

THE VIGIL OF DISCLIPLINE

At some point, I realized that marriage requires determination as well as discipline. Not the kind that makes you get up at the same time every morning or stick to a fitness routine, but the discipline of knowing what is true and right, as well as not allowing false ideas or false people to interfere with that. It is the discipline of hope and of believing in the goodness of man and woman. It is a discipline of spirit that seeks to guard against the voices of fear and doubt which are secretly perched high up and out of sight. Like a vigilant mother of a tender new baby, you must guard your marriage's sweet *Sakinah* and preserve her precious beauty and innocence.

SOUL MATES

My daughter once asked me if her father and I were "soul mates." I responded quickly that, unfortunately, we were not. I told her that, as I understood the concept of soul-mates, these were heavenly matches that are exceedingly rare. I said that soul mates are perfectly matched in every respect; having the same thoughts, enjoying the same things and cooperating with such synchronicity that their lives seem to be joined as if in a single stream of easily guided energy that flows peacefully from one soul to the other without interruption.

My marriage, though blessed abundantly, certainly did not fit this description. While in most areas my love and I are well matched, in other ways we are utterly incompatible. Although we love to spend time sharing ideas and dreams with one another, at other times there are barriers to communication that are so severe that we withdraw inwardly—as if having concluded a silent agreement to conserve precious energy rather than waste time trying to convey any thought or idea to the other. While energy levels do flow smoothly at times between my spirit and his, connecting us as if in one mind, there are times when severe electrical storms cloud and corrupt the trust that is needed to restore our universe to its precious calm. "No," I repeated to my daughter, "your dad and I are not soul mates because that kind of relationship and state of relatedness is very, very rare."

Some days later, I recalled our conversation and began to think that I might have been wrong. Perhaps soul-mates were not perfectly compatible in all ways. Could soul-mates also be so when two souls are brought together by G-d to assist and inspire the other towards achieving their own highest personal destiny? Perhaps soul-mates are best designated as such, when they are challenging one another to forgive, grow, repent and change. When I explained this to my daughter, she smiled in her special way—a smile that informed me that she agreed with me completely and that she'd known this already.

"DANCE"
You better dance, girls! All I can say is you better find some meaningful music, and rise up and dance! You can take a class or two to learn a few steps and some turns, but this is not necessary—no, not at all. All you need is your own body, your own feelings, your lessons and stories. And know that with every agile move of your hips you strengthen the life-line; with every contraction of your stomach, you improve your ability to carry the weight that the gift of life requires that we all carry through time. Lift those legs and speak with your arms and remember, with every graceful sway of your hips, you strengthen the life-line! Teach your daughters to dance also, so that they might learn those things that you cannot find the words to say. Teach them to breathe, balance, and focus. Tell them to sing out the joyous, truthful and grateful words to life's songs. Tell them that we women must dance in mind and body and spirit to keep the world connected, loving and strong.

INNER VOICES
It is exceedingly important, in fact vital, that you develop the ability to identify and manage your inner self and inner voices. If you are not in touch with your hidden, subconscious conversations, you will likely find it difficult to arrive at the tranquil state that your soul is craving. When we are in touch with those thought patterns that drive our moods and decisions, we are more capable of achieving inner peace and also, of relating productively with others. This is especially important for marriage. You will find it invaluable that you learn to force your inner workings to the surface so you can present your best and most authentic "self" to your husband.

If you can be still and quiet enough, you can hear the subtle voices that make you who you are, as they are always operating. You can practice isolating these core beliefs and conversations by asking yourself some key questions. How do you feel right now about yourself and about the life that you are constructing for yourself? What are you thinking about your future? What are your beliefs about G-d's plan for your life and destiny?

You will likely find that there are healthy aspects of your personality that tend to trust completely in your human excellence and value, while there are other aspects of your thoughts that may be doubtful and self-condemning. To improve your ability to manage your inner self, you should consciously place your best mental attitude in charge of your inner conversations. You should also allow this voice to have the final word just as you would expect a loving parent to have the final word after an important discussion with her children.

During these "conversations," notice which thoughts and feelings are operating when you are afraid, worried, excited, or when you desire something very strongly. These feelings must be expressed if you are to realize the true underpinnings of how your mind is operating. To further get in touch with your underlying beliefs, ask yourself if you view The Creator as being caring and sensitive to your life and needs, or do you believe subconsciously that G-d is harsh, indifferent, vengeful, or unforgiving? Get a sense as to how you tend to respond to your thoughts and feelings and whether, through it all, your thoughts are validating the true excellence of your human essence.

You will find that the careful reading of the Quran scripture is the very best way of developing the ability to manage these voices in the most productive way. This is true as long as you are reading the Quran with a heart that desires good for all. It is vital to read the Quran through the lens of mercy—the perspective that firmly believes in G-d's Unyielding Compassion to His entire creation.

Indeed, G-d suggests that it is through this lens that the most accurate meanings of scripture are comprehended.

Remember that, as you are discovering your subtle, inner thoughts, you are empowering yourself towards becoming a completely integrated human life force. With this, you will be far more capable of relating to others with integrity and will empower yourself to make far more valid life decisions.

LISTENING

One of the best gifts that a wife or husband can give to one another is taking the time to really connect with what the other person is saying by listening. In listening, you let your love know that his thoughts, ideas, feelings and dreams are important to you. Your listening skills can develop to the extent that you can hear beyond the details, and into the essence of what he is saying. So often the things that we say are, in some way, designed to achieve validation, just as much as they are designed for imparting information. Hopefully, your husband will also listen to you as you share your experiences, seeking comfort, validation and support. Furthermore, as you are speaking you should try to listen to your own motivations, so as to discover what you are really trying to achieve through your communication. This inner listening is the best way of arriving at solid conclusions with respect to how to handle the emotional implications of any particular situation.

REMEMBER

G-d's Blessed Love and Mercy is continuously being showered upon you. Remember also that G-d's Love towards humanity is perfect, flawless, sincere and incorruptible.

MODESTY

Modesty is expressed in your clothing, yes, but it is also expressed through your humility and kindness, as well as your desire to have mercy for yourself and all others. The consciousness of modesty knows that G-d's love extends to all of His Creation. In the spirit of true modesty we do not seek to disturb the peace or dignity of any other human being.

COMPANIONSHIP STYLE
We are different as human beings in so many ways, so it should come as no surprise that we express our needs for companionship differently. He may like to cuddle all day, while you feel easily smothered and desire more than anything the gentle touching of hands. Hopefully, if you have differences in this area, you will both learn to stretch just a little towards embracing your love's companionship style.

THE EXPERTS
There will be books—such as this one—articles and findings that will seek to advise and inform you as to what you should or should not do in your marriage. Some of the advice will be helpful and some, you will find, simply does not apply to you and your husband's unique lives. Ultimately, you must learn to trust yourself. G-d has invested you with the ability to think and reason and to be able to hear and understand His blessed answers to your prayers. There is never a time when "expert" advice should supersede what you know in the deepest recesses of your heart and soul to be right and good and true.

TOUCH
It is documented that we human beings gain great physical and psychological benefits when we receive massage or therapeutic touch. I have read that when one *gives* a massage, the massage-giver's body experiences some degree of healing in the same locations where they have massaged the other person. Touch sends powerful mind and body healing substances that improve physical health

as well as mood. These biochemical substances are the same ones that pharmaceutical companies attempt to simulate or trigger in creating antidepressant medications. Touch aids us also by improving our sense of feeling relaxed, loved, and cared for. Take the time to touch your love with a casual, gentle stroke or with a complete healing massage. When you need the same healing of the laying-on-of-hands, simply make the request of him.

OVERLOOKING

Almighty G-d—Highly Glorified is He—advises both husbands and wives to overlook the faults of their spouses. At the same time, G-d acknowledges and informs us that our spouses and children can be the cause of hardship or trial for us. Now, I am not going to tell you that overlooking the errors of your love will be easy, no indeed. I can, however, verify the soundness of this advice. It can be a little challenging when you have sensed that your ability to overlook these faults can be mistaken for your not caring. This is captured by the classic "taking one's kindness for weakness" scenario. Some things should be overlooked and just forgotten, while it seems that other things need to be overlooked with some degree of conscientiousness. To combat this when necessary, I have developed the method of lightly informing the offender that I am aware of the misdeed, yet I have *chosen* to overlook it. I try to do this with a sense of humility and humor.

MOMMY

I am finally understanding the value and meaning of many of the life-lessons that my mother attempted to impart to me. Whether or not you have had a good or a strained relationship with your mother, you are likely to perceive her life more fully as you walk further down the road of marriage. If you become a mother yourself, this awareness will again expand. I try to send my mother little notes of acknowledgment and gratitude to let her know that I love her for her sacrifices and her words, and that I really do finally understand.

YOU

I pray with all sincerity that you are seeing you. I pray with all my heart that you are cherishing you. I pray with all my mind that you are educating you. I pray with all my soul that you are sharing you. I pray with all my compassion that you are forgiving you. I pray with all my love that you are loving you.

THE QURAN

The Quran is literally the "you" manual. With it, G-d provides us with food, water, medicine, and purification. The Quran's guidance heals the human social life, as well as the individual human psyche. The Quran provides comfort and purification with fire and light as it cleanses air, water, and earth. When reading through the lens of a sincere and humble heart, we are reconnected in its pages with our noble human ancestry, and with our excellent human worth.

READING

There is so much to learn and to know! In every direction there are information feasts spread out for you to partake in. Our Prophet Muhammed often mandated that Muslims continuously be engaged in the pursuit of purposeful knowledge. We should celebrate the fact that we are blessed to be living in a time when there are abundant viands for improving oneself in every aspect of being human. Married life is great for companionship; yet, marriage also provides a wonderful setting for enjoying more private time. This is true especially if you have never lived alone or if you come from a large family. Enjoy this time of being free to read whatever interests you, and to catch up on reading that you promised yourself that, "one-day," you would certainly do. If you become a parent, you may find that you can never seem to learn enough to carry out your parenting duties, so this is also a great time to read about pregnancy, childbirth, and parenting.

Understand also that the reading of the printed word is only one type of reading. You can read the sounds of a rain shower or the brightly speckled, whispering petals of a flower. You can read people as well, observing moods and postures and all sorts of non-verbal cues and body language. Reading allows you to explore the world with a celebratory heart while discovering some small part of the vast meanings of life, death, and renewal.

TRUE LOVE

I have noticed that in the English language there is a subtle distinction between the concepts of "love" and "true love." I am puzzled as to how there could possibly be any difference between the two. Is the use of the word "true" designed to project some sort of oath or vow as to the validity of "love?" If this is so, then the word "love," standing alone, would seem to be somehow imperfect or flawed. Thus, the idea of "true love" makes simple "love" appear corrupted or corruptible when unqualified by the word "true."

Perhaps "true love" refers most accurately to the perfect love that the Merciful Creator has for us, His prized invention. In this light, the word "true" would not signify a qualification for the validity of love, but would instead advise us as to the purest source for the origination of all love. "True Love," used in this way, could be used as another expression for the concept of G-d, as all love is in some way reflected from this perfect love. And, G-d's Love can never be diminished, even by our limited exploration of the experience and awareness of love.

Thus, when we believe and trust wholly in The True Love, giving and receiving love for G-d's sake only, then our mortal love is always perfectly true.

IDIOSYNCRASIES

How my husband puts up with my idiosyncrasies, I do not know. I also feel sometimes that I should be pinned with a medal for putting up with his. I can be very particular about many things, especially when it comes to germs. This, however, can't be helped as I am a mother and also trained as a nurse. Additionally, I can be very particular about other things, such as not being able to drink cold beverages from coffee mugs and my requests that my sandwich be layered with the flavors of certain items placed in a certain order, so as to affect the location where a particular flavor hits the palette. I am also somewhat idiosyncratic about my husband putting on fragrances in our room when I am asleep. My first pregnancy increased my sense of smell one hundred-fold and I haven't been the same since! Well, anyhow, you get the idea. I like things to be done just so.

What complicates matters is that my love also has his own peculiarities and idiosyncrasies. His desk must be perfectly ordered without a single paper on it that is not his, and under no circumstances can anyone wear his socks! I personally find this one to be a bit excessive, but what *is* important is that we are, at least, aware of each other's pet peeves and try to accommodate one another as best we can. Stay flexible during the getting-to-know-each-other process. Enjoy your love and good humor and you'll both be fine.

PERSONALITY

They say that there are an estimated twelve to sixteen basic personality types. The study of personality always reminds me of the Quranic stories about The Children of Israel who could each recognize their correct spring for drinking water. Like these tribes, we all tend to gravitate towards those with whom we share the most things in common. There was a time when it was thought that opposites were best matched. While there might be some truth to this, it is widely believed that relationships fare better when we share critical common characteristics with our spouses. However, whatever your personality type, if you are both respectful of the same source of guidance, you can resolve differences and keep a sound course.

One of the things that I love about personality analysis is that it helps couples to resolve potential conflicts before they have a chance to start because it allows us to view a person's actions through a helpful lens. If you are extremely sensitive to visual things, for example, a slightly disheveled room might be really disturbing to your peace, whereas a person who exists more in their mental space might not even notice this. Rather than make character judgments about one person being oversensitive, under-sensitive, sloppy, clean, etc., we can simply understand that the other person actually perceives the room differently. It can actually be as if one person is always wearing a high-powered magnifying lens, while the other is wearing a lens that leaves many of the details of the room a blur. Whether or not you ever actually do a personality analysis, you should take the time to study your partner and get to know his sensitivities so that you both can get along better.

VICTORY
There are times when your rightness about a matter will be manifest quite significantly. Keep in mind, however, that the mark of true refinement and beauty is to win humbly and graciously.

SPIRIT MIRROR
Sometimes, we think that marriage can provide a safe haven for us to run away and hide, as if our vows will allow us to become hidden in the deep forests of a newly sheltered life. I have, however, discovered this to be an illusion and false to the extent of irony. The truth, in fact, is very much to the contrary. Marriage will not provide even a moment of shelter to you from the work you must

do with respect to becoming alive as a whole and purposeful human spirit force. Rather, marriage will place you directly in front of a soundly crafted spirit-mirror that forces you to discover and uncover things and reasons about yourself that you could never before have known. With this, also, you will be challenged in your spirit to fight hard at seeing what is true, real and right. And yes, your mirror will yet yield bold and lovely angles—in addition to well-lit views of the beautiful spirit of the woman that you have become.

COUNTING DAYS
Now we, as educated Muslim ladies, are undoubtedly aware that when we feel offended we are allowed up to three full days of silence, indignation, and withdrawn passings before being bidden to forget and let go of another's past wrongs. We also know instinctively, that if it is sadly discovered that we have been wed to a secret "Pharaoh," we are wise to peacefully slip away, as Moses did, back to momma and daddy's, or to some other safe place. Yet, we are hesitant to reserve these same full three days to serve, celebrate, or simply listen to our love. I too am guilty of counting off far too few days while having this abundantly fruitful perception.

TRIBULATIONS
I wish that I could shelter you and myself, as much as possible, from the hardships of life's difficult trials and tribulations. Inevitably, though, life exposes us to necessary pressures as we are tested in our capacity to become enlightened with respect to our inherent human suitability for the garden. As you walk through life's struggles, please know that the remembrance of G-d is the greatest force in all of creation and that the very thought of G-d can dissolve mountains! Hold on to G-d firmly and, if you forget Him, simply bring yourself back just as soon as you are aware of your absence. Don't waste time

with guilty feelings. Remember G-d with frequency and force; and whenever you are delivered, remember to give your wholehearted thanks and praise only to Him.

THE LABORATORY

Many years ago, a very dear friend of mine who'd been married for several years before me advised that young brides should look upon their marriage as an exciting new laboratory that can be the setting for all sorts of exhilarating and meaningful experiments. She would say that each day presents a new opportunity to explore some meaningful area of your relationship. When looking at married life in this way, one doesn't see setbacks as personal failures but rather as experiments that need to be adjusted and tried again, using different elements or performing them under slightly different conditions or with different calculations.

As a young bride, this advice armed me mightily. I had such fun trying new things, being a new wife, and bringing new experiences to our days. We savored candlelight dinners, inexpensive travel, giving small parties, and our own private meetings. However, things took a rather stark turn when I became pregnant for the first time. I was catapulted into a world of sickness and total inactivity. My state, I am sure, utterly shocked my husband. I could hardly get out of bed, the mere sight of food rendered me dizzy, and our apartment was a terrific mess! I was grateful, though, that we'd had those times of special fun so that he could at least look forward to getting his new bride back one day.

PLEASE

The use of the word "please" is wisely employed by all who respect and value kindness and decency. Its use shows appreciation for the energies and efforts of the person asked from the very outset. Its use also reflects grace and humility. The same is also quite true when it comes to the use of the words "thank you."

CYCLES
It is quite normal for marriages at all phases, to go through cycles or seasons. Both you and your husband will likely find that your interests are continually shifting and adjusting as time progresses. In times when you are going through normal cycles of internal change, continue to enjoy one another's company as you explore how you are feeling. Also, give each other space if necessary. You are both constantly adapting and becoming new people, as well as becoming invisibly stronger and visibly more mature, so be patient if the relationship needs an occasional restorative nap every now and again.

THE BODY
It is reported that Muhammed has said that our bodies have rights over us. This says that we cannot ignore the legitimate needs of our bodies. We need clean air and water, as well as foods that are wholesome and lawful—*Halal.* We also need to stretch, strengthen, and challenge our muscles daily—especially our hearts—by engaging in some type of aerobic activity. Get regular medical and dental examinations and listen to your body's communications, paying attention to changes. Don't be afraid to address concerns or have something unusual checked out. Conditions that can be healed easily, if addressed early on, can become complicated if left to linger. Be aware that our worries and fears can actually inspire disease as well. In the end, trust wholly and completely upon G-d's love, as this Trust is the wellspring of all healing.

ELDERS
I have found my life to be tremendously blessed when I am able to spend time with elders. Making time for the

elders in your family, and those within your community, can be one of the best things that you can do for your soul and marriage. Elders are "living history;" they are also the manifestation of an abundance of well-learned experiences. Even when seemingly debilitated, elders teach us important new lessons as to how to care for one another in kindness. These lessons serve to preserve us in the truest picture of our humanity.

YOUR SMILE
There is no better gift than this to offer or share with him, whether offered in the morning, when he arrives home from work in the evening, or at any time, anywhere and for any reason.

ASKING
There is a very interesting phenomenon that often occurs between husbands and wives once bound together in the same home. We sometimes expect our love to know things, as if by magic, without being told. It appears that we become obsessed with the notion of having our minds read. I, too, suffer from this malady as I say that I don't care what I am given for my birthday, only to complain later on that I expected my husband to know somehow that I *really* wanted something else. Sometimes I don't ask for specific things because I sincerely don't want to burden him. However, this past Mother's Day, I forewent these mind games, deciding instead to offer accurate information as to my true wishes. As you have probably guessed, this time I received the gifts that I truly wanted.

It may seem to be more romantic when we are given gifts that are quietly selected by a loved one who has secretly mastered the knowledge of all of our secret desires; yet, in today's hectic world, it can be extraordinarily difficult for husbands or wives to figure all of these things out independently. I am learning slowly to let go of the notion that I am somehow helping my husband by not asking him exactly for what I really want. Communicating your desires affords your husband clarity; it also provides him with tangible goals to reach for.

MONEY

It is often said that most disagreements and breakups in marriage are over money. I believe that there is a great deal of truth in this statement; however, this idea may also be somewhat misleading. Sometimes we think that this refers only to the challenge of having a lack of money, but this is not necessarily true. Money issues are super-charged because money has become the symbol of our sustenance and success on so many levels. We see personalities revered, not for possessing good character or their G-d consciousness, but, rather, because they are "rich and famous." In contrast, we find that there are people who possess very good character and demonstrate extraordinarily generous support for charity, yet may be distrusted, prejudged, or criticized simply because they are wealthy. It is understandable that money creates such strong emotion because all of our vital needs seem to be, in some way, tied to its presence. The experience of lacking material needs is also seemingly determined by money's absence. The truth, however, is that all sustenance flows from G-d.

Like the powerful Pharaoh, the material machinery of modern living has put forth a paradigm so compelling that all but the very strongest of minds find it difficult not to fall under its hypnotic sway. Muslims, however, are invited to live under consciousness and respect for G-d as the source of all bounty. We trust also that we, as ordinary mortal human beings, are capable and worthy of receiving such abundance.

Additionally, Muslims should take care not to subscribe to theories that are premised upon the notion that resources are fixed and limited. Indeed, G-d revealed to mankind over 1400 years ago—in the Quran—that the universe is actually continuously growing and expanding. This does not support the idea that Muslims should ever waste resources. We are, however, to appreciate more than anything, the invaluable resources of our human excellence and our productive human intellect. We trust that G-d has given mankind the ability to utilize the earth to supply the needs for all of humanity. This reality is manifesting itself to us continuously with the technological revolution and the modern "digital" age.

Muslims need not be afraid of money. In fact, G-d enjoins that we claim our share of the material world. Rather, we should always keep in mind that a share of all wealth belongs to the weaker members of the society. As we face the responsibilities of acquiring and managing our resources, we should find abundant inspiration within the lives of great visionary minds, such as Abraham, Moses, Jesus, and Muhammed—each of whom successfully challenged the prevailing culture in some way so as to establish strong, healthy community life. To this end, we must rekindle the courage to see money as a tool for man's use, not as a source of our identity or human value in any way. We should strive earnestly to create abundance so that we can care for our loved ones, feed the hungry, and supply much needed healthy Islamic education.

MANAGEMENT
Husbands and wives who have a healthy relationship with money are not afraid to manage their resources on a weekly basis. They set goals and create a budget, and are able to step "outside the box" and view money differently. They seek money not for the image that it gives them, but for the work that it can do for achieving good. They know that money is soil for planting great ideas that serve humanity.

DISCOVERY

It is said that "life" is actually that which is unfolding while we are actively involved with making other plans. This makes us aware that we can sometimes be so driven by our need to reach for our desires that we forget that, with each and every day and stage of life, if we are living sincerely and consciously, we are already whole.

RATIOS

Some years back, I read a report based upon a study which confirmed that a marriage's strength and longevity could be predicted based upon the ratio of certain positive cues when compared to negative ones. I believe that the ratio of positive cues to negative ones was 6:1. This meant that couples more likely to have strong marriages were found to be very prone to doing and saying little subtle things that communicated their love continuously. Negative cues and comments were not completely absent in the relationship; however, the negative cues were strongly outnumbered. I absolutely loved these findings because they supported a marital culture of being demonstratively affectionate, which I personally liked, and also gave couples some easily applicable, concrete tools for strengthening their marriage. Furthermore, this advice was in accordance with some other advice I had received from my good friend Sabreen after she had experienced her second divorce. She advised me to take care to give attention to the "little things." "Big things don't break up marriages," she advised, "it's always the little things."

There are scores of little things that you can do to communicate love in subtle ways. A sweet glance, a smile, a squeeze, a stroke, a small gift, or even a bag of favorite chips—these all communicate the language of love to him. And, if you find that you have inadvertently done or said something that he may have perceived as being negative, take care to counter these actions by offering plenty of kindness and loving deeds or gestures, so as to repair the damage and to also provide future inoculation.

LOVING LOVE
I think it impossible to love any man if you do not love goodness, kindness, beauty, and love.

GIZMOS, GADJETS AND "THINGS"
If you are not already aware of this as a result of living with your own father, be forewarned that many men tend to really love gizmos, gadgets, and "things." This affection for "things" is a source of great enjoyment for many men. It is easy to appreciate man's affection for new technology, considering that technology has brought him such vividly beneficial results for survival. We should remember that simple things, such as the wheel, although now taken for granted, were at one time phenomenally important, brand new, life-altering technological advances. We can only imagine the sensations of wonder and excitement that the early man must have experienced when discovering new tools for preserving food or for hunting. Considered in this light, men's engagement and preoccupation with "things" is actually a monumental gift to the human family.

Now, having spoken of the positive aspects of these tendencies, we might also look at an alternate view. First, the practice of collecting "things" can become seriously problematic when those things are a source of debt, waste, or clutter. Furthermore, reining-in the activities of any man who is given to collecting gadgets and gizmos can be a daunting task. The reality is that we live in a time when advertisements and cultural influences are particularly adept at exploiting the male's inherent, technologically focused tendencies.

One solution might be to agree on an amount allotted for his use towards making these purchases. This obviously should be calculated in accordance with what you can reasonably afford. If you are not yet a homeowner, this fund should probably be small as, far too often, monies used for playthings, if saved, might make a very respectable down payment on a home.

This said, you might find that some of his things are really useful even to you. In fact, right now, I am using a wonderful notebook "toy" that my love insisted on buying against my better judgment. Now, his toy and I are almost inseparable and I actually use it far more than he does.

KINDNESSES
The words of the Quran are invaluable insofar as teaching us the value of small acts and words of kindness. We are advised that a good word is like a good tree whose roots are firm and whose branches reach to the heavens. I have witnessed this ever so often in my life with friends and family, as well as with my husband. Be sure to see small acts as re-magnetizing the world towards goodness with silent atomic force. Do not wait for *thank you's* and don't try to measure results. Simple courtesies such as a smile or small offers of concern—all serve to re-align those hidden forces that are secretly and quietly recreating the Garden.

DEMANDS
Could it be true that we ladies have lost the delicate art of making the strictest of demands, while leaving him with the impression that we were humbly and gratefully asking?

GRATITUDE
When he has received some kindness from you—of course, if he has not already done so—request with girlish playfulness and charm that he show his gratitude by saying "thank you." You are reminding him, not on behalf of your own need to be thanked, but as a result of your sincere desire to aid him at winning as a humble servant of G-d.

REST AND REJUVENATE

You are no martyr, my dear, when you engage in the act of neglecting yourself. In fact, you are demonstrating the severest cruelty and harshest unkindness when you refuse to allow yourself to have adequate rest and receive other means of gaining physical and mental rejuvenation. There is no nobility or spiritual benefit in allowing yourself to give up so much of yourself to others that you are feeling dissipated and constantly unwound. Eventually, your exhaustion will harm the very ones for whom you are sacrificing yourself and wanting to give so much of your love.

Resist the urge to give up everything of yourself to others. This urge is a natural female tendency but, in our stressful, mixed up world, this can become a lethal female condition! Give yourself small gifts, such as putting yourself to bed at night rather than falling off to sleep while you are in the middle of doing everything. Eat breakfast in the morning, and practice sitting for some minutes while slowly sipping a warm cup of tea. Make time in your day to allow your heart to fill back up: seeing your spirit as one with the universe in honorable service of The Great Majesty.

RECREATION

Primal fascination with your new life as a newly wed wife may seduce you into forgetting that your mind-spirit is alive, separate and apart from your husband's. A symptom of this condition can be seen when subtle resentments begin to stir that call for your husband to spend more and more time stimulating and entertaining you. This calling for life and stimulation may actually be your own voice, in your own mind, speaking out its needs to you. The voice may be saying "You used to do things that made you happy on your own" or "You used to learn new things and give time to the community." This voice may simply be calling for you to return to the life of feeding and nurturing your own unique soul.

DATING

Make regular going out "dates" with your love and try to keep this as a married-life tradition. These dates will become especially vital later on if you have children. Let go of burdens for these hours. Allow these interludes to be light, and learn to leave the never-ceasing business of your marriage behind you as if blowing in the wind.

SPEAKING

Learn to speak to your love through all of his senses and not just with your words. Some men are more attuned to olfactory cues rather than auditory ones. They are quick to notice fragrances or odors of any kind. Other men are more attuned to visual input, such as symmetry and colors, while still others are more sensitive to touch. It is well known that men are spoken to also by what they taste, as stated in the adage, "The way to a man's heart is through his stomach!" In addition, be conscious as to what type of sensory input is most likely to appeal to you.

THE NECESSITY OF NAGGING

Don't worry too much about engaging in the practice of nagging your husband. It seems that whether wives are gentle and subtle or straightforward with suggestions, husbands often consider any effort to correct or help them see something differently as "nagging." Males can become very strongly attached to doing things their way and even if logic suggests that something should be done differently, they sometimes "dig in," insisting on doing a particular thing the way that they want to do it. I am of the opinion that there is not very much one can do about this. You are not doing him or your marriage a service by failing to bring accurate information to his attention, and no matter how delicately delivered, he may seem to be unwilling to listen.

Believe it or not men *do* listen, even when they are putting up a huge fuss, so you gain nothing in attempting to guard his ego by not seeking to correct the situation. It is important to realize that men instinctively "listen" for intent and motivation, so as to protect themselves from attack. Therefore, you should try to make sure that your mood is friendly, warm, and perhaps a bit humorous.

Try to bring matters to his attention adeptly and gently without undue or prolonged emphasis or suggestions that his method is "wrong." And, please don't bother waiting around for him to openly surrender or submit to your advice. Simply deliver the information and then leave it alone. Let your attitude and mood be light. You are simply sharing information. I find that this technique is less likely to trigger a "digging in" reaction. Furthermore, if you are requesting that some action be taken, it is always nice to flavor the request with some small treat for his ears, such as "honey," "sweetheart," "darling," or whatever special love-name you normally use that makes him feel cherished.

The fact is that you are his partner. He needs your help and you both know it. Just try to be kind and respectful so his soul can recognize yours as one that is always committed to protecting him with your love.

COMFORT
Do not hesitate to offer tender words of comfort to your love when he has experienced some disappointment. It isn't necessary to fix the problem; just be there knowing, and letting him know, that G-d's love is with him.

COMPLIMENTS
There is probably no single better way to inoculate your marriage than to offer to one another sincere compliments. Notice those little things that reveal your love as being a special person and praise them. "You look really nice today." "You smell wonderful." "You played a great game yesterday." "I agreed with your analysis; it was right on

point!" If you have a good thought about him, share it; don't keep it to yourself. There is no need to make things up, just be observant and aware. There are so many things that you admire about him; this is surely one of the strongest reasons that you married him.

BLESSING HIM

I don't see how this could be true, but it is so. I feel ashamed to admit this but for many years I didn't think very much about praying for my husband. How could it be that the person closest to me, whose biggest struggles were largely engaged upon on my behalf, did not register as being in need of my prayers? On any given day, there were multitudes of other people and causes that I would find myself praying for, so how could I neglect to pray for the person whose goals and dreams I knew and understood so intimately?

I think that, at this stage, I hadn't yet perceived that my husband was vulnerable and human like me, or that he too, was still in the process of "becoming." I somehow didn't connect to the awareness that he also needed protection, light, and strength. Or perhaps I simply saw him as my protector, provider, and maintainer, while forgetting about him as a sacred human soul.

To make matters worse, as it turns out, during this very same period my husband was always in the habit of praying for me. I know this because he would often tell me so. He would also let me know that he made daily prayers for members of my family. I cannot say for sure when the light went on in my heart that reminded me of my husband's need to be prayed for, but I know that when it did, there was so much more fulfillment and happiness between us and in our marriage. It is odd the way husbands and wives can regard each other, sometimes seeing one another as continuations of themselves rather than as separate, whole souls.

Now, my prayers are always including him. I pray for him when we are apart and when I am with him. I pray for him when he is asleep next to me and when I am in his embrace. I pray that G-d will protect him, strengthen him, guide him, and forgive him. I pray that he is blessed to have all the good things he desires and that, in facing any disappointment, G-d will comfort him. I pray that G-d will help me to become a better wife to him and also a better mother to our children. My prayers flow openly and sincerely now. These prayers are sometimes accompanied by tears as I ask G-d to please aid my husband and shower His blessings upon him.

CONSULTATION
It can be very tricky indeed to get good advice about specific problems for your marriage. You want to preserve your husband's privacy, yet you need to get clarity or guidance so as to resolve important issues. The best consultation I have found is that which is achieved through prayer. Parents or trustworthy married friends who are committed to marriage would be the next best choice. It is still always best to protect your husband's privacy as best you can just as you expect that he is protecting yours.

TRADITION
One of the most satisfying joys of being married and raising a family is establishing or cultivating family traditions. Traditions preserve the values of what a particular family feels and thinks should be held up as being most important in the lives of its members. Traditions also bond us with one another in a very beautiful way, so try to remember those things that were particularly meaningful, fun, or special in your family gatherings and celebrations, and continue doing them.

REGRETS
You will have them. Make amends, and trust that G-d is abundantly forgiving.

RESENTMENT
Try not to keep a scorecard, because the building of resentment is like allowing infection to fester within the body. There is no place for resentments to drain and they will come oozing out at every possible opportunity. If your husband makes a mistake and then makes amends, let it go. If you can't easily forgive him, then ask G-d to remove and empty out any lingering hurt or resentment that you may be harboring. This prayer should also include the cleansing away of resentments that you may be storing up against anyone else who may have harmed you, be it a parent, a past partner, a stranger, or a friend.

MERCY
When I extend mercy to my love, or to any person, I hope and pray in earnest that G-d is accepting my act of mercy as cause to forgive me for some of my own faults and sins.

YOUR SIGNATURE
One of the best things about being in your own space is that you are finally able to express the shades and nuances of who you are apart from your parents. At home, you may not have had the ability to decorate your room just as you would have liked, or your parents simply may not have had the room to store your budding art collection. Now that you are on your own, you are finally able to express yourself in your space. You can sign your name upon the world, as you are now uniquely your own woman.

LOVE NEST
Creating your love nest is about making your home feel safe and warm as if elevated above all troubles down below. You are also creating a clean and orderly space that

serves the needs of your family. Families thrive in such environments, especially when the truest pulse beating through your home is the pulse of trust in G-d's Perfect Love and Majesty.

TRUST

I wish that there were some method that I could use to create some sort of halo or perhaps some golden shimmers of light around the word "trust." I wish this, so that all could see how important the concept of trust is to marriage and, indeed, to life itself. Truly, all bonds of civilization are established upon trust, and the very future of human existence is promised to those whose trust in G-d is purified. There could be absolutely no safe human coexistence had we not been imbued with a strong tendency for being trustworthy and for trusting in one another. Sometimes, I think that the very foundation of matter on the subatomic level is actually captured within the simple command of the word, "trust."

The ability to trust in G-d completely is most essential. It seems there is some mysterious bond between man and G-d that can only be alluded to by this concept, for that which is created is only truly safe when held in the trusted presence of its Creator. Trust first, that G-d our Creator, does not want or need to harm us. In fact, G-d wants to see us fulfilled to our best and highest potential, whose boundaries are only comprehended by Him.

Trust that every relationship that G-d has blessed you with is a gift towards improving your soul and making you more worthy of the unimaginable joys that He has in store. Trust also that the man you love is an excellent soul, also capable of reaching his highest human potential with the Grace and Mercy of G-d and also, trust that your marriage can be superb.

Your marriage is not your mother's marriage or your friend's marriage. This relationship is a gift that G-d has selected just for you. Trust, therefore, that even if you err,

G-d will never leave you. Why would He have invented you with the potential to make mistakes, only to then condemn you eternally for erring? This is not to justify sinful or shameful behavior. This is said, rather, as a tribute to the superior human quality of repentance. Remember that repentance is acceptance. Trust that G-d still believes in you always and that with His aid, you and your marriage will win!

SCHEDULES

Some people find schedules to be confining. I believe, however, that schedules are liberating. Without some measure of planning for your day's activities, your time is threatened beyond reason. I once had as my obstetrical patient, a Saudi princess. The princess was pregnant and needing some specialty care, and I had the pleasure of caring for her. Despite common stereotypes about wealthy people being wantonly lazy and spoiled, she was very serious in her devotion to Islam and she greatly valued time, as was evidenced by the schedule that she maintained. While she did have several assistants, this did not inspire her to waste her time. Instead, she employed a very competent assistant whose responsibility encompassed keeping her schedule running smoothly. While you may not be able to employ someone to keep your life running smoothly, you can construct a clear plan for how you intend to spend your day.

There will, of course, be times when the very best schedules are seized upon by surprises, emergencies, and interruptions. Still, if you have a schedule, you can at least have some map that can guide you back to your desired course. Without one, you are simply lost at sea!

SYSTEMS

It is absolutely necessary to establish sound systems for running your home as smoothly as possible. Time invested here at the outset will save you a tremendous amount of time later on. You should institute simple mechanisms for keeping important documents, as well as photocopies of documents and identification, secure. You should also institute some simple logical system for filing and/or storing important receipts, payment records, school related documents, warranty documents, bills that need to be paid, mail, coupons, recipes, magazines, catalogues, and books. In simple terms, you need to create a good filing and paper management system. Good labeling is absolutely essential to any serious paper management system because everyone in the household needs to know exactly which things are to be used for what task, and where they belong. Be aware that storage solutions can also be incorporated into your decorating scheme, for example, creating scrapbooks and photo boxes.

A laundry and clothing management system should be decided upon. You also must have some menu, meal planning, and food storage system in place. These are the basics. You will, of course, develop your own unique systems, but they should at least incorporate the above concerns. Otherwise, you will likely encounter major problems running your home later on. Also, don't hesitate to change methods if something isn't working for you after testing it out.

THE POLITICS OF OBEDIENCE

It may not be politically correct to speak of being obedient in these times; however, if the truth be told, it is a rare woman who doesn't absolutely love the idea of cooperating completely with a husband whose judgment and character are of such caliber that is worthy of her obedience. Muslim women, however, are counseled in the Quran continuously to remain obedient to the commands of G-d first and foremost. Still, most women I have encountered from any faith tradition are not in the least concerned about accepting the authority of a good man when final decisions pertaining to the safety or viability of the family must be made.

From a practical, as well as a legal standpoint, it makes sense that males have the final authority in decision making in the home. This is because, if the family is seriously stressed or negatively affected by any given decision, males must ultimately bear the burden of protecting the family's interests. Women, historically, have not been as capable of doing this, as they are the traditional bearers, nurturers, and caretakers of small children.

Muslim families are the recipients of a progressive democratic system known as *Shura Baynahum*. This ideal refers to the practice of "mutual consultation" that is firmly mandated by the Quran and was employed consistently by our Prophet Muhammed. The Muslim leader is advised to canvas the members of the community for the best solutions to solving those problems and challenges that the society is facing. We are to do this without regard to race or status. We are also aware that, with the advent of Islam, women were afforded rights to vote, own property, and freely address their concerns to the rulers or the prevailing government. With such a rich culture of inclusion, Muslim husbands are wise to administer their homes in a manner that speaks to the brilliance and distinction of the early, authentic Islamic socio-political structure and traditions.

TIME

For marriage and for life, be conscious of the value of time. According to the Quran, time is not on our side, unless we are given to trusting faithfully in G-d, as well as being active in the doing of good. Furthermore, it is said that we should be focused on encouraging one another in doing what is true and right, while also encouraging one another in the practice of perseverance.

POSSESSIVENESS

If your husband is very doting and protective of you, consider yourself blessed. Occasionally brides say that they feel their husband's attentiveness as possessiveness. They may also feel a little smothered. His insecurities may be coming from some deeply embedded psycho-spiritual place, so it might help to talk to him about what fears are interfering with his trust. If there are serious problems, you might suggest some counseling, but don't focus too much on this, unless his behavior is really extreme. This tendency will likely dissipate with time.

Instead, try to relax and focus on establishing those foundations in your marriage that build trust. Remember that resisting his need to secure you may only cause him to tighten his grasp. It might also help to find joy in his attentiveness, perhaps even bragging about his protective nature just a bit, as this might let him know that you really do value this masculine aspect of his personality. Understand that your husband's nature commands him to guard you. This is programmed into him by Almighty G-d. While you might feel it is a nuisance, it is much better to feel protected and cherished than to feel neglected and unloved.

BEING RIGHT

Many years ago, my brother asked me if I knew the difference between being "right" and being "righteous." He apparently sensed that I would be in need of this important information for the rest of my mortal life. "You see," he explained, "you can be *right* about something in perfect detail, while your intention in bringing forth the information is not *righteous*. You can deliver information that is completely accurate and truthful, while at the same time possessing no sensitivity whatsoever as to how your words are making someone else feel." He further asked, "Do you think that G-d looks upon us with more favor when we are being *righteous* or when we are simply being *right?*"

MASKED MAN

Some men are very complex and complicated, and not easily seen, for reasons that are also well tucked away and hidden. You can prod and attempt to psychoanalyze this man with questions about his mother or his father or past hurts and pains, and you can also attempt to heal him. You can try to steal a peek at his true self, perhaps even capturing his essence for a quick, fleeting moment—only to find that he has adeptly retreated safely back into his private world, well-hidden. I truly know no way of unveiling such a love without allowing discovery to come with the passage of time and the shared work of building a good life with him.

SHIPS PASSING

I hope this will not occur too often with you, yet I would be remiss if I did not forewarn. There may be times when this man who you love so deeply and tenderly can be so distant in his ability to comprehend what it is that you are saying. At times, when even the simplest things cannot be communicated accurately; it may almost seem as if he simply doesn't want to understand what you mean. Best-laid efforts to clarify your meaning may only serve to confound and confuse both of you more completely.

How frustrating it is when these discombobulated verbal engagements occur. "How could you think that I meant this when I said that?" and "No, I did not say this; I said that!" Perhaps both of you are too preoccupied with other thoughts and feelings, or some hidden insecurity may even be the culprit, as we watch these two ships sailing in deep fog, sometimes nearly colliding. It is just as well to allow these failed attempts at communication to pass. Just let them go. These lost opportunities seem tragic; yet, inevitably, you will return to one another, some time in the future, when clearer skies are on the horizon.

THE FEMININE
It is no wonder that virtually everything that is sold or touted as valuable is marketed via some aspect or symbol of feminine beauty. There seems to be no limit to the intrigue and interest that the human psyche possesses for capturing the ideal image of femininity. While bold depictions of women as seductresses stream from the airwaves and from glossy pages, today, men seem that much more starved for the real food of femininity. They seem to crave a safe and secure place to share their ideas as newly planted seeds; they seek the perpetual flow of warmth, wisdom, intelligence, and morality that spills over from your heart intoxicating their minds while satiating their deepest yearnings to be whole and complete.

AUTHENTICITY
Be yourself in your marriage and in all relationships, but know that your "self" is still growing, learning, stretching, reaching, and becoming. The human soul is in the process of becoming until we are free. Authentic "you" has so many expressions and shades; you are a daughter, a friend, a granddaughter, a cousin, a wife, and perhaps also a mother. So keep on striving to persevere in your authenticity. That is the self that is becoming everything that G-d has given you the potential to be.

DUTY
This word is not popular these days, yet, where would humanity be without this principle? The sense of duty that parents have towards children and children feel towards their parents is essential to our society. As dutiful wives and husbands, we are to keep the agreements that we make with one another and we should fulfill those tasks that must be fulfilled in order for our lives to run smoothly. To

be dutiful towards one's spouse is to treat him with the utmost respect and to operate honorably towards him. Duty also implies that you are trustworthy. Although there is certainly nothing wrong with serving the needs of another person, the ideal of duty suggests that we are serving a *principle* rather than a human being. It implies also that we are working for the sake of the whole rather than for any individual.

Husbands and wives must both be determined to uphold their sense of duty. With this, we acknowledge that, in marrying, we have undertaken a sacred responsibility—one that cannot be shaken off when we are simply not "feeling" the other person or even when we are not "feeling" our own selves. As a married lady, you must be committed to protecting the vital needs of your marriage. Furthermore, keep in mind that your sense of duty to marriage should extend far beyond your own home. When your marriage is healthy, you are also helping to preserve the beautiful and blessed pattern of life that G-d has chosen for all of humanity.

FREEDOM

The excitement of being in a new marriage can be so filling that you don't sense any loss of freedom at all. This may not, however, be the case. Oftentimes this loss of freedom is completely self-imposed. The slight sense of having lost some of your freedom can be remedied by making a firm commitment to continuous self-improvement in some way, everyday. Take a class, learn something new, and make time to bond with family and socialize with good friends.

MALNUTRITION

A young bride complained that she nurtured and nourished her husband very, very much and very, very often, yet the more she gave, it seemed the more he demanded. His need for care and attention was endless, and he was always wanting more of her attentions. This new bride felt emotionally wasted from all of this seemingly endless giving. A wise elder lady informed the young bride that, although remaining somehow previously undiagnosed and undetected, this new husband was clearly afflicted with a very tragic hungering condition. This, it seems, was a manifestation of an untreated case of emotional malnutrition. She said that it would previously have been wise for the bride to have fed him on small spoonfuls of porridge and sips of bland liquids. Alas, this window of opportunity was now past. And, now that this husband had tasted the good food of her love and care, he was now understandably intoxicated by love's exciting colors, delectable flavors, inspiring aromas, and rich textures. But the past is the past—and besides, this malnourished husband would very likely have eventually arrived right back here in this same severely wanting condition.

The older married lady then commenced to offer the young bride her expert medicinal opinion. "The skill now, my dear, is to carefully begin to educate your poor husband as to the art of serving, nurturing, giving and feeding. He might learn these lessons quickly, if you can at the same time learn to simply start gently *requesting*. Now, my dear, when he has fed you any small morsel, you must raise your voice and spirit very high, in honest, joy-filled appreciation. With arms opened and eyes lit with gratitude, your sincere gladness will serve as his best medicine. Keep in mind that you are duty bound in these things you must teach him…so that he might know how delicious life can become when one is giving rather than receiving."

CIRCLES
It is reported that our Prophet Muhammed stated that women are curved like the rib; and therefore should not be pressured to become straightened or might, thus, become broken. I believe this metaphor suggests that Muhammed

appreciated the fact that men and women should understand they are different and that, by nature, men and women utilize different modes of thought processing. Muhammed's comments also clearly direct men not to attempt to change the inherent nature of women. Muhammed's selection of the rib to strike his comparison is said to be a reference to the understanding that women are naturally inclined to protect the vital organs of the heart and lungs. I have heard it said that in this context, the heart is a symbol of the social ties that bond us together; the lungs are symbolic of our spiritual life (we are informed by G-d in the Quran that at some point during gestation, G-d "breaths" something of His spirit *"Ruh"* into each one of us).

A great deal of research has been concluded which supports the idea that males and females do process information differently. The female brain is unique in that it supplies many more sites of connectivity between the right and left hemispheres than does the male brain. Perhaps this is why, as most husbands would likely affirm, the female brain never seems to "power down." It is as if there is always some kind of conversation going on within a woman's mind. We are constantly integrating information across the right-left brain divide, enabling women to process lots of information and details all at once. Furthermore, women tend to be much more adept at communication and being empathetic than men are. All of these abilities are extremely useful when it comes to educating, nurturing, and safely managing the energies of our offspring.

Another extension of the unique aspects of female brain physiology is our sensitivity for keeping social connections intact. We are more likely to want to visit a relative or to accept a social invitation so as to uphold the emotional ties that bind us to one another as a society. Women are that structure within society that curves as it protects the heart as we ensure that the circle of family and friendships remains intact and unbroken.

Men tend to operate more specifically on one side of the brain when performing any single activity; thus, they do not communicate as proficiently across the divide. They are, however, able to subject a single matter to intense focus and analysis and they are more skilled at handling many unrelated tasks at the same time—multitasking. It is also said that males are able to actually give their brains a rest, which, in effect, provides their brains with a "time out." This might be viewed as the same energy-saving rest state our computers cycle into, when not needed for high-level functions. Thus, when the male's brain *is* "powered up" to meet a challenge, he is able to accomplish wonders without expending the same type of resource-draining energy as do women. It seems that G-d is calling forth this powerful aspect of the male brain in the Quranic description of males—*dhakara*—as "thinkers." While G-d makes it clear in the Quran that women are "thinkers" as well, the Quranic term for female—*untha*—points to women's highly developed sensitivities.

Despite these categorizations, some men have developed the ability to process information adeptly and quickly on behalf of a sense of universal social responsibility, sensitivity and spiritual focus, in the same way that is characteristic of women. Indeed, the Prophet Muhammed seems to have been such a man. Perhaps this is why Muhammed is referred to throughout the Quran as possessing a kind of "mother intelligence" rather than any formal education. We see this in Muhammed's persistent inclination towards broad scope concerns that included every member of society without regard to race, gender or nationality.

It should also be noted that Muhammed's inclination towards being sensitive to the needs of others did not in any way disable him as far as being a very masculine man. For example, although Muhammed did not want fighting or war, when Muslims were forced to defend their fledgling community against ruthless persecution, Muhammed was the bravest general, leading his men into battle and fighting right alongside them. However, in keeping with his balanced nature, he did not allow bitterness, rage, or vengefulness to cause him to violate the high principles set forth in the Quran for defensively engaging in battle. Muhammed was also foremost when it came to seeking reconciliation among opposing factions as soon as such opportunities presented themselves. As if always seeking to restore peace, he tried to keep intact the circle of humanity.

PROTECTING HIM

We are instructed by G-d that men are charged with maintaining and protecting their women because—generally—men have more access to wealth than women do. The Quran, however, also advises wives to protect their husbands. Wives are instructed to guard in their husband's absence that which they would have be protected. We know that we are to protect our children, our modesty, and our good reputations. Wives are also to protect the family by protecting our homes, property, and other important assets in any way that we can. However, having said this, we are sometimes unaware of the protection that husbands need from invisible invaders, such as stress, distractions, and anything else that threatens to harm their health and safety.

We might also stretch this idea to the understanding that we sometimes must protect a husband from himself, as can be the case during times when stress might be causing his judgment to become distorted. It is in this spirit that you might prepare fresh fruit or a healthy dessert for your love rather than continuously serving him the richest ice creams or all of the sweets that he desires. Your actions might make you a little less popular with him in that particular moment, but he will at least know in his heart that you truly care about him. If your husband does not desire such protection, you are not held responsible. Still, you should always attempt to act as his trusted and true friend.

CONTRACTS, VOWS AND COVENANTS

In the Islamic faith, marriage is considered as a legal contract. Vows are taken in public as a witnessed contractual agreement between a woman and a man who are equals. The contract details are also written and signed, as is the case with any other legal contract. Interestingly, in the traditional Islamic wedding, the vows are worded in such a way that the woman is actually making the marriage offer, as was the case with the Lady Khadijah. Prior to the development of a formal Islamic community, Arab women were largely considered as property and, as such, did not often engage in legal negotiations. Islam created a new social structure that allowed women to be respected in all legal matters.

The Islamic tradition also provides for a Guardian-Advisor or *Wali*, who is put in place to act as a legal advisor and intermediary for the woman. Traditionally, the *Wali* was specifically provided so as to protect the interests of brides who did not have a father or another male family-elder to advise and protect them in this most important negotiation. Naturally, under normal circumstances the bride's father is her *Wali*. While some might remark that the necessity of a male guardian reinforces the idea of male dominance, this argument is not reasonable. Prior to Islam, the vast majority of women had not historically been educated in negotiations and had previously been excluded from business matters. It would have been unfair to suddenly give women their independence without instituting some solid measure for helping them understand how they were to utilize it. Just as contemporary businessmen are in the habit of hiring advisors, the *Wali* is an advisor, charged specifically with protecting the bride's interests.

In the past, the presence of the *Wali* also served as a means for protecting young women or girls who were orphans from somehow being coerced into a marriage they did not want. In modern times, even in cultures where women are well educated, the *Wali* serves as a buffer between the man and the woman. This provides a means of protecting women's privacy and modesty, in such intimate dealings with men.

The Islamic dowry tradition is established as a payment or gift of some kind given by the man to the woman. The negotiations with regard to the dowry should be performed in consultation with the woman's Guardian-Advisor. The bride is allowed to keep this gift regardless of the outcome of the marriage, as long as the marriage has been consummated. The woman is free to use this gift as she pleases. This practice serves to restrain men from marrying any woman as a selfish whim. Men are hereby forced to view the marriage from the outset as a very serious investment. The practice of offering the dowry also serves to provide women with their own resources, perhaps in compensation for the traditional home-life work that women have most often done without adequate compensation. Women are given the freedom to excuse the dowry if they so choose and their husbands are allowed to enjoy this gift heartily if it is thus returned.

Despite the fact that marriage is considered to be the most vital aspect of Islamic tradition and community life, we are seeing a very interesting phenomenon occur among some Muslims. In some cases, dowries are set so high that marriage itself has become a prohibitively exorbitant endeavor. This is truly a sad occurrence, especially considering the many advisements that are reported as given by our Prophet Muhammed, one of which cautions: "Those who do not marry are not of my community!"

While the details of the marriage contract are legal matters, there are many aspects of this endeavor that are far more important than can be expressed, even by a legal contract. Due to the fact that marriage can produce helpless children, we should take great care to choose wisely and well when we are in the process of selecting a husband. This decision will certainly affect you and your entire family permanently. For these reasons, once married, we must strive to uphold those responsibilities that G-d has asked us to maintain as husbands and wives. We should seek to perform our best in our marriages—with far more enthusiasm, diligence, and focus than we do when we are studying in school or working towards a career or professional goal. When we take our marriage vows we should perceive our words as assisting, upholding, and strengthening the entire human community. We should keep our duty to the *ideal* of marriage as our personal covenant with G-d, taking it seriously, while also thoroughly enjoying the great blessing that G-d has afforded us.

THE DOWRY
Get what you can, my dear ladies; indeed, offer skillfully and get as much as you can! Take counsel with your Guardian-Advisors and then make your solid and spirited demand. Yet, if priced much too high, you may be left caressing only your offer, rather than your man.

SUPER MODELS
It is often true that the women in our lives who have served as the best role models—as women, mothers, wives and career mentors—go largely unnoticed. Meanwhile it appears that we are always celebrating and noticing the women we view in the media. I grew up surrounded by some amazingly beautiful ladies and have drawn greatly upon my experiences among them as a wife and as a woman. These women have been from many faith

traditions and they have all touched my life in very distinct ways. They include the gracious Christian women in my family and community who nurtured me, the excellent Christian and Jewish teachers who educated me and of course, the phenomenal Muslim women who generously shared their love, practical advice, and stunning insights into spirituality. All have served as superb models for me as a woman at some stage of my life.

I was raised by my maternal grandparents who stepped in to support and assist my mother in raising my brothers and me while my mother pursued higher education after she and my father separated. Despite the separation from my mother, there was no shortage of motherly influence in my life. I was blessed to spend a great deal of time with my maternal grandmother, two great-grandmothers, several "aunts" and numerous neighbors who were like aunts to me—treating me like their own family. These neighborhood women were mostly the mothers of my childhood friends. And, although the stereotypical media depictions of African-American life portrayed an abundance of single family households, of all the families that I knew and grew up around, I was the only child who was not being raised by her two parents. This served in some ways as a great blessing because many of the women of my neighborhood, surely out of pity, often took me into their homes and under their wings.

My next-door neighbor, Mrs. Drew, was a very devout Christian lady, as were many of the women in my community. Her home was kept immaculately and, as she was from a large respectable family in Virginia, was filled with southern charm. Mrs. Drew and her husband were a very kind, old-fashioned, young couple. Mrs. Drew took care of my hair at the request of my grandfather, because my grandmother was not particularly skilled at hair care and she was extremely busy. My hair flourished under her care. And, while sitting in that chair down in her basement,

Mrs. Drew would dispense loads of advice that served as guidance. "Stay in school." "Don't mess around with those boys." "Stay out of trouble and get your education!" Mrs. Drew would always fill me with words of caution as to what she knew could lead me astray. She was somewhat strict, but I could tell that she liked me. I also noticed that Mrs. Drew kept her combs and brushes very clean and she always tidied up thoroughly after she performed any household task. When she went to church on Sundays, Mrs. Drew was always stylishly dressed and she exuded such an air of sophistication. In my mind, I always saw her as being the African-American Jacqueline Kennedy Onassis.

Mrs. Hansen was my Girl Scout leader. She was also a friend of my mother, as they had attended undergraduate school together. Mrs. Hansen's speech and diction was perfect. I had been trained to notice these things because my mother was a speech-language pathologist. Mrs. Hansen was tall and graceful looking, just like a fashion model. She raised her two daughters with certainty and seriousness; so, while we were allowed to have fun and play, Mrs. Hansen's presence informed you that she did not tolerate foolishness. I enjoyed going on small Girl Scout day-camping trips with her family. I also enjoyed spending hot summer days playing in her pool. Mrs. Hansen always acted respectfully towards me. This, in turn, motivated me to want to behave respectably around her. I have found being exposed to Mrs. Hansen's countenance very valuable to me as a woman and as a married lady.

Mrs. Munford lived two doors down. Her daughter, Norma and I were inseparable. She had a warm, friendly smile and she was always inviting me to go somewhere with her entire family. While her husband was very serious, Mrs. Munford had a playful, happy presence that gave her a sort of girlish charm. I often went to church with her family and they encouraged me to sing solos to their congregation. Mrs. Munford would also caution me very often with regards to the things that I should and should not get involved in. She let me know that she thought I was very intelligent and that she expected that I would one day do important things. Mrs. Munford's kind words of love and support remain with me to this day.

Mrs. Roker was also a gentle, loving influence upon me. She raised her children as strict Catholics and always demonstrated a strong love for children. She and her husband seemed to be very much in love and their home was always full of humor and warmth. Sometimes, the Rokers also carted me off with them to their church to receive Holy Communion. Mrs. Roker once saved me from significant personal humiliation after I showed up at an annual "Red and White Ball" wearing a mauve and crème-colored dress! My mother hadn't had time to shop because she was working so hard. Mrs. Roker skillfully diverted the hostess' attention away from me as she quietly explained my unique home circumstances. When she was informed that, disappointedly, I could not be allowed to participate, Mrs. Roker graciously sheltered me for the rest of the evening.

Anne was my closest neighborhood "aunt" and, although older than my mother, for some reason we were allowed to call her by her first name. Her daughters, Helena and Annette, and I pretended to be cousins and we got away with it because both our families enjoyed strong friendship ties from "the good old days" when they all lived in Brooklyn. Anne allowed me to spend the night at their house for seemingly endless weekends. Her demeanor was serious yet very loving and Anne had a very healthy sense of humor. With her quiet smile and humble demeanor, she was ever willing to listen patiently to me when I had a problem. My brothers and I always felt that when we needed someone, she would be there to support us.

Interestingly, all of these women, who were either practicing Christians or Catholic, continued to be gracious and good to me after I converted to the Islamic faith. Not one of them ever did nor said anything negative about my becoming Muslim. In fact they continued to be friendly, supportive, and positive. Some asked questions about my choice then, as if satisfied that I had made an informed decision, continued to be kind and gracious Christian women.

Mrs. Swygert was one of my high school guidance counselors and she was a tremendous support to me during a critical time in my life. My choice to become a practicing Muslim (at the age of thirteen) had not interfered with my success in junior high school. In fact, a completely non-Muslim—predominantly Caucasian— student body elected me as student government president. However, when I went to high school I experienced a great deal of isolation. During this period, my mother was going through some major life transitions of her own and my grandparents were having serious relationship difficulties. It also was very difficult for me to juggle the culture shock of going into a school building with thousands of students, as opposed to the smaller school settings that I was familiar with.

Being an African-American-Muslim in the mid 1970's—a time when very little was known about Islam within the mainstream American community—was very challenging as well. On one occasion, a very large gang of Caucasian male students, all clad in black leather "bomber" style biker jackets, attempted to intimidate me by blocking me from entering the school while making taunting comments about my faith and my Islamic attire. Thankfully, I knew how to handle these types of situations with confidence and humor rather than outrage. Nonetheless, these types of occurrences were extremely emotionally taxing.

While some teachers seemed to be very confused by my Islamic attire and head covering, Mrs. Swygert seemed not even to notice. Instead, she relentlessly pursued her mission of organizing the minority African-American student body to provide them with opportunities to become exposed to African-American history and culture. I never confided in Mrs. Swygert about all of the difficulties that I was experiencing at home or in school, but her office became an invaluable oasis for me. I absolutely relished the opportunity to assist her in her mission.

I am sure that during the years that Mrs. Swygert was helping me to cope, she had no idea how difficult my private life was and how much her leadership and kindness meant to me. Her example has taught me to try to reach out to young people, whether or not they seem to need any help. I am keenly aware that, very often, those who need support the most are the most hesitant to ask for it.

There were so many other women whose lives modeled decency and beauty for me that I wish I could write about each and every one of them. I must, however, reserve some space for mentioning the influence of the Jewish teachers that served as models for me, especially in my early formative, grade-school years. These teachers were so wonderful to me, especially considering that my brothers and I were often the only African-American students in the school's "Intellectually Gifted" classes. I recall them as being strict and well prepared, and I also remember how very seriously they took their work as teachers.

I especially valued that we were in no way patronized due to our "minority" student status. Our teachers spoke often about the civil rights issues of the day and they were very much in support of the work of the anti-Vietnam War movement. They also insisted that all of their students demonstrate empathy towards their fellow man. I recall that one of these teachers liked to quote an adage that my granny also kept posted as a plaque up on her wall: "Never condemn any man until you have walked a mile in his moccasins." On one occasion, after having performed at a B+ level on an exam, one of my teachers called me to her desk and insisted that I work harder, saying that, from me, she would only accept excellence. In this academic environment, I felt loved, valued, and capable. I learned from these teachers to insist upon justice for all people, and to challenge my own children to continually strive for excellence.

PROSPERITY

It is interesting to note that poverty is considered a lack of *Sukun,* which refers to rest, calm, solace, or quiet. This seems to suggest that when you are tranquil and quiet within your spirit, you are free to become truly wealthy.

CHANGE

Many couples find at some time in their relationship that there is some behavior or attitude held by their spouse that they would like to see them change. These issues can become very serious and they can be the cause of a great deal of marital conflict, perhaps because change is such a very personal matter. Most of us prefer to make adjustments only *if* and *when* we choose to do so—even when we know that the prospective changes are likely to be positive ones. Perhaps this is why we are advised by our Prophet that the greatest *Jihad* is the one that is waged within oneself for self-correction.

The science of change is, in so many ways, the essence of the human experience. While we as human beings are seemingly flawed due to our natural tendency to move towards the earnest pursuit of our curiosities and yearnings, we are informed by G-d that we are actually His chosen *Khalifah,* or His custodians—created to care for, and inherit, the entire Earth. We as humans are also endowed with an amazing ability to make corrections and to improve upon ourselves. This quality seems to be the one that sets us apart more than any other, from the rest of the creatures of the Earth. Still, we can be very reluctant to make changes unless given the right motivations.

If you feel that your love would really benefit from making some kind of change, you are obligated as a Muslim to make this known to him. If he does not accept your invitation, then you have done your part. Employ patience and try not to trigger a battle over the issue. Very often, when a male's "battle mode" biochemistry has been triggered, he becomes driven to "win"—even when the "winning" is not in his best interest.

It is probably best to simply overlook your husband's unwillingness to make changes, except when change is absolutely necessary in some way for providing protection or benefit to the family. If this is the case, there can be serious difficulties when one's partner is unable or unwilling to make adjustments. In such cases, there may be a need to seek assistance from family members. G-d instructs that we invite a person from each family to assist in arbitrating these kinds of serious matters.

It is absolutely necessary to pray for G-d's help for the healing of such circumstances as they can be the source of great discord. It is also valuable to remember that the word "Muslim" holds the meaning of "one who surrenders, peacefully." There is an implication within this title that we be willing to make valid changes for the sake of keeping or preserving the "Peace" that G-d intends His human beings to have. With this, we are invited to be resilient and to be ever ready to make adjustments based upon what is rational according to G-d's revealed plan. Also, keep in mind that, while you cannot control another's actions, you can always make changes within yourself. If your husband is reluctant to make adjustments, your demonstration of having the ability to compromise can serve as an example for him.

It is reported that Muhammed stated that the best action is the one that is performed consistently. With this, one thinks about making small changes in one's life rather than sweeping radical changes. So, if your husband shows any small willingness to make any adjustment at all, be appreciative and supportive and try to give him some time and space.

FOOD HANDLING

It is amazing that, considering the amount of damage that can be caused by lack of proper handling of food, food-handling education is not covered in most school's curriculums. Be aware of how you handle raw meats, raw fish, and uncooked eggs; be sure to clean/sanitize adequately and wash your hands thoroughly before and after handling these foods. Preparation of all other foods should be accomplished in such a way so as to avoid any contact with these potentially contaminated foods. Take care also, to separate the utensils used for raw meat, raw fish, and eggs; be sure that these foods are cooked adequately enough to kill any potentially harmful microbes. Additionally, all preparation surfaces and utensils should be cleaned thoroughly with hot water and some type of antimicrobial or disinfectant cleaning solution. It cannot be stressed strongly enough that all family members learn how to handle food safely in the kitchen. This is especially important for the health and safety of babies and the elderly.

YOUR KITCHEN

It is said that the kitchen is the busiest room in the home, so there is good reason to try to organize your kitchen right from the beginning. Keep in mind that items should be stored near the area(s) where they will be used. Also, try to always keep your work surfaces clean and uncluttered.

Be realistic as to how you use your kitchen and plan accordingly. For example, if you tend to sit at the kitchen table to pay bills, you might create a space in your kitchen area to organize related items like stamps, envelopes, pens, etc., Most importantly, make your kitchen safe. Clean up oil spills in ovens and on stovetops immediately. Keep a fire extinguisher on hand, and be sure that everyone in your home knows how to use it. Try to make your kitchen functional, inviting, colorful, and warm, as it is the place where you and your entire family will likely spend most of your happiest moments with one another.

SAFETY
Both you and your husband should take a basic First Aid class as well as CPR training. Stay abreast of home safety recommendations and make it a habit to read the manufacturer's safety instructions on all new products (no matter how boring or unnecessary this might seem). Install smoke detectors and carbon monoxide detectors in your home immediately if you do not have them already; and check them at the beginning of every month—or as often as the manufacturer advises—to make sure that they are in good working order. Whether you have children or not, it is wise to childproof your home to some degree because you never know when a friend or relative with small children will be visiting.

EFFICIENCY
I am somewhat of a stickler for efficiency, although this is not to say that my home always runs as smoothly as I would like. I do, however, absolutely love having the ability to discern which method would be best for accomplishing any particular task quickly and effectively. The arrival of children into your life and home will surely sharpen these skills and you may also become more sensitive to these concerns if you and your husband both work or are otherwise very busy. While there are loads of

marvelous references to help you gain skill at performing common tasks with greater efficiency, there is no match for common sense applied with a few moments of careful analysis.

Be aware that there may be times when efficient living seems nearly impossible, as was the case when I lived in a house that was continually undergoing some type of construction or home improvement project. We tried our best, but being organized was truly difficult during this period. Also, as you create systems of order for your belongings, accept the fact that you may have to experiment a little before coming up with the very best strategies for your family.

MUSIC
The Islamic wedding does not traditionally incorporate music into the initial part of the ceremony where the contract/vows are affirmed—*Nikkah*. This tradition respects that there is never to be any type of coercive influence upon any person when entering into a legally binding contract. In Islam, all serious legal decisions are to be decided upon, and entered into, based upon each party's free will, sound reasoning, and careful thought. However, after the vows are concluded, Muslim families usually stage a very festive wedding celebration—*Walima*—where good music and good food can be enjoyed.

I think it is always a good sign if you and your love share similar tastes in music. Meanwhile, it is also fun to expose one another to musical genres that the other has not yet learned to appreciate. My husband and I both enjoy listening to many positive and inspirational musical artists in all genres of music. We really love jazz, be it swing, be-bop or contemporary, as well as the soul classics and classical music. However, while my husband has developed a penchant for several kinds of Rock, along with some Hip Hop music, my tastes diverge more toward some of the classic Pop music that was popular in the 60's and early

70's. I tease him about his musical tastes, but have actually become exposed to some very good, new music through him that I have truly come to enjoy. When we have the time, we find listening to music to be a fun and inexpensive way to share time together.

QUIET

A very dear sister-friend once advised, "Cherish your mornings, as morning-time is very special." As she, too, is a mother of seven children, she would often share useful advice with me and I have always found myself feeling blessed in listening to her words of wisdom. With this advice in mind, I try to capture some of the still and quiet of the morning just for myself each day and I have found this practice to be very restorative.

I also love experiencing quiet time in the company of my husband. I am quite sure that he cherishes these occasions as well, because I, like many women, can often be very chatty when I am bringing him up to date on the goings-on of my day. On days when we are both very settled or when we both have our own personal work to do—be it reading, writing or simply thinking—we can spend hours together in one another's company quietly living in our own separate worlds, while still immensely enjoying being in one another's presence. These shared quiet times are truly marvelous. I believe this to be the *Sukun* state of existence that G-d has intended for all marriages to experience. It is difficult to attain these times of quiet when we are worried, stressed, or insecure within our own being. Therefore, these occasions must often be consciously carved out or "intended," so that we are aware that we do not want other outside influences to interfere or threaten them.

Truly, the most compelling quiet times for me are those that are experienced in the stillness of the night, just before the arrival of the wee hours of the morning. It was stated by Muhammed that these are the most sacred times for offering special prayers. The quiet of night invites us far inward into vast areas of self-discovery and prayers offered during this special time are said to be blessed tremendously.

WELCOMING HIM

I believe that there is a delicate art as to how to welcome your husband home. This can be very personal and it is different for different men. While I often like to slip back into our home silently without my children noticing too quickly that, "Mommy is home," my husband tends to like his presence to be verified. As such, I try to be sure to offer him a sincere and warm welcome home. However, once welcomed, he often needs time to find his internal space, so I try not to seize upon him by offering too much information all at once.

COMPLIMENTARY

Compatibility, of course, does not mean that you and your husband will be alike in all areas. This ideal refers more accurately to your having similar dominant personality traits, while also enjoying shared goals and aspirations. Compatibility also allows for the idea that we can be very well-matched with someone whose skills and strengths are different from our own. In fact, our differences may actually serve us in many practical ways. As a species, we are more likely to survive when mated with those whose immune systems are different from ours. In everyday terms, this means that your husband may be able to perform certain tasks that you don't like, or are unable to perform; conversely, you might be delighted to fulfill some function that would be a great burden to him. Thus, these "differences" are making your family more effective as a whole. In this way, variations in personality can actually be of benefit. Learn to see your differences as having the potential to serve your relationship, as long as those differences are complimentary.

BETTER THAN EQUALITY

I was dismayed when they failed to pass that amendment calling for women to be compensated with an equal salary. I felt so, until I realized that G-d had something much better in store for us, and this something is spelled: T-E-C-H-N-O-L-O-G-Y. Soon, we will be able to work from almost any location on G-d's spacious Earth, and we can all live more abundantly.

EQUALS

In the Quran G-d informs us that we—males and females—are created from "one soul." G-d further categorically describes the nature of man and woman as being equal before Him. In these times it is difficult to imagine the cataclysmic changes in the perception of women that were brought forth with the revelation of these values in the Quran. At that time the ideal that women were to be regarded as equals within their households and communities was extremely radical. Muhammed was regarded as a madman and a nuisance because of his teachings regarding the Oneness of G-d and the equality of all human beings. It was considered that such a religion would amount to no more than a passing fad.

In its earliest years, Islam served as a tremendously major force on behalf of equality for women and humanity in general. Indeed, Muslim women who lived in the community of Muhammed enjoyed advancements rarely seen by women prior to Islam's arrival. In fact, Muslim women of the early Islamic civilizations in Baghdad and Spain were the most liberated and well-educated women in the world! It is important for us to remember that for the Muslim woman, equality is not simply to be regarded as a political right; it is her G-d ordained inheritance.

YOUR PEN

Your pen will surely prove to be your mightiest tool for creating a life of order and fulfillment. Write out a daily plan in a book that also has a calendar. Prioritize your plan and begin your day by doing those things that are top priority first. When you make appointments for anything whatsoever, make note of this on your personal calendar and your home calendar as well. Your daily organizer can also be used to keep lists and to jot down brief memos. I keep notes of important phone conversations, as well as a written record of most of my other daily encounters, in this book. There are several planner-type books on the market. However, I have found it most useful to create my own planner using a blank, lined journal. I like these kinds of journals because the pages are usually bound firmly. Avoid using spiral-bound books or books with perforated pages because they are likely to come out. I also prefer to use a ballpoint ink pen rather than pens with gel or any other liquid-type ink as they are more likely to bleed if the pages inadvertently get wet.

ALWAYS AND NEVER

It is ridiculously funny to me now to think that, prior to getting married, I felt that I needed absolutely none of the—then popular—marital advice about how married couples could learn to argue productively. I seriously believed that my love and I would never, ever have the need to argue. Why should we? We shared the same faith, dreams, and goals. What could there possibly be for the two of us to argue about? Now, I believe that not only is there much for a married couple to potentially argue about, marital success seems to correlate with *how* we choose to argue. My lack of preparedness for handling the inevitable disagreements that relationships normally experience left me very severely handicapped in this regard.

When my husband and I had our first disagreements, my mind would become so full that I could hardly think at all,

153

let alone think clearly or purposefully. Now, after almost thirty years of being in a relationship with my husband, I am still learning the rules for disagreeing productively, yet I would have been much better prepared had I, at least, acknowledged back then that this area of marital life was an important one needing consideration.

When emotions are running high or you are feeling vulnerable, try to quickly create some mental space between the part of yourself that is involved in the dispute and the part of yourself that is a loving, parent or friend towards all human beings. Next, try to isolate in your mind what the two points of view are really about. Focus on the issues and how the other person's point of view or actions are making you feel, rather than focusing on your husband as a person. Allow your inner-parent voice to be in charge rather than a voice that is driven by vulnerability or fear. When the vulnerable "you" must speak, make this voice speak truthfully as to your feelings. Sometimes, to that regard, a simply stated fact, such as "You have hurt my feelings" is sufficient to get the conversation back on track. "I" statements are even better, for example: "I am feeling hurt because…" It can be difficult to be honest about your feelings, yet this can save so much wasted, misdirected energy.

Be aware that some men have the tendency to release their frustrations about work or personal disappointments on their wife, as she is often the one person that he feels he can be "real" around. If your husband has this tendency, it is imperative that you withdraw from his emotional sphere of influence as soon as you are clear that this is what is going on. Your withdrawn mood and reserved demeanor must clearly communicate that you are a cherished lady who is not in the habit of being spoken to, or treated, in an unkind manner—especially when you yourself have done nothing wrong. Believe it or not, this can be effectively communicated without you actually speaking a single word.

When you are engaged in any difficult discussion, avoid using words designed to reflect a diminished view of your husband's character or his essential humanity. It is said that when we are tempted to use the words such as "you always" or "you never," this should be a signal that we are straying away from managing the issue at hand towards the realm of character or personality assassination. Cruel words said in anger can be later apologized for; however, this certainly does not mean that your love will ever really forget that you have said them. These negative events can cause couples to begin constructing invisible walls of distrust which can eventually become almost impossible to climb or conquer.

PRAYERFUL

I cherish the times when I am able to offer any of the five formal Islamic prayers—*Salah*—together with my husband and family. Often, busy schedules threaten our ability to offer the daytime prayers together. Nonetheless, there are tremendous blessings to be gained by families when we pray together. When families pray in congregation, invisible bonds of love and commitment are strengthened between them; this extends outward in such a way that the entire Muslim community is blessed. I also encourage my family to pray deep within their own minds throughout the day, continuously giving thanks to G-d, while also praying for the concerns of all others who are experiencing some difficulty within their hearts. In keeping with the practice of Jesus and Muhammed, I try to pray for those who have wronged me as well. I learned this lesson well from my husband's Aunt Virginia, who is a lovely Christian lady. Many years ago, she somehow gained the strength to separate from a violently abusive husband, yet when she speaks about him she still manages to bless him!

I recall that I would often find my great-grandmother Mary sitting alone in her room for hours at a time. "What do you think about while sitting in here all day long,

Grandma?" I would ask, following this question up with continuous offerings to take her out to *do* something. I thought that I was rescuing my great-grandmother from what seemed to me to be a life of terrific boredom. My great-grandmother's usual response was that she was *"already busy*, sittin' in here prayin'." Indeed, my great-grandmother took to prayer as if it was a highly salaried vocation as, in truth, did most of the women in my family. Now, as I have grown more aware of the tremendous challenges faced by so many people in our world, I too have found myself relying on prayerfulness as a tool for serving humanity as well as guarding my own peace of mind.

Dear Sakinah

My dearest sweet *Sakinah*,

How excited and happy I was when I first heard the joyous news of your engagement!
I couldn't help but to recall that it was not so long ago that you were just a tiny, newly-born infant.

And, I have watched you blossom happily from a bubbly and cuddly baby,
Into becoming a sweet, delightful, little girl, and now a charming and vibrant young lady.

Yes, you are a woman now, all grown up and yet still growing on.
And soon you are to marry. I simply do not know where all the time has gone.

Sakinah, there are so many gems that I wish to share with you about marriage and love, I feel I don't know where to start.

I'll say first that these jewels can be held by no hand, but rather only by your heart.

And just as countless others have aided me through all sorts of new situations,
I am now passing on these treasures to you, to be shared with future generations.

These lessons are culled from the sittings-in on the labors of women who taught me what it truly means to pray,
Women who have loved, cherished, and nurtured me so that I might help prepare you for this day.

Now, some of these women you must surely remember, but let me help you try to recall them:
Do you remember, *Sakinah*, when you encountered for the very first time, all of those amazing Muslim women?

How they taught you to love and to trust and to live in consciousness of G-d?
You said that those sisters seemed to know just about everything! And that they worked extremely hard.

Like Nisaa Muhammad, who always instructed you with such refined and focused wisdom.
And Lily Adams Muhammad and Emma Suluki and Aahirah NuMani...*Sakinah*, do you remember them?

They were so devoted as they taught and prayed and cooked and sewed and then marched off diligently to all of those important meetings.
All so that one day you might lay claim to your sacred intellectual freedom.

And I hope you can recall, *Sakinah*, how those ladies loved you up, indeed how they loved all of the children.

Yes, they loved you all something powerful, and they truly loved their religion.

And do you recall how you trembled when you first heard the story of sister Clara's historical confrontation?
When you learned that she told those officers she'd "die as dead as that door facing!" before she allowed her Muslim children to be given an ungodly education.

And you understood, even as a young girl, that Clara Mohammed's compelling drive to offer her husband some new words of hope and inspiration,
Was surely a catalyst for the rebirth of an entirely new nation.

I remember sadly, also the day, *Sakinah*, when you walked somberly out onto the street determined to pray over dear sister Betty's coffin,
Saying "Had it not been for Betty Shabazz's devotion to her husband's work, G-d only knows where we Muslim women might have been."

I am sure that you will remember all of these sacrifices, my sweet *Sakinah*, but please recall a few things more:
Like how you stood at the house built by Abraham in Mecca, just a few nights before the war.

Do you remember all of your sister's lovely and pious and innocently brilliant faces?
They'd traveled there from nearly every city on the earth, some from very remote and distant places.

They came from Turkey, Malaysia, and England, and also from Nigeria.
They came from Ghana, China, Iran, and Switzerland, and some from Albania.

And then there was that Palestinian grandmother who said that she lived in Jordan.
And the Iraqi sister who wept long in your arms in *Al Medina al Munawwara,* when you said, "I am American."

How you held the memory of all of these women within your heart as you prayed on the plains of *Arafat.*
How you prayed for them and their families with all of your might. My dear love, I remember that.

Now, I hope that you don't think that I wish to fill you with indignation on these days before your wedding.
No indeed, my dear, to the contrary, that is not remotely where I am heading.

I wish rather, to fill you up with pride, and hope and jubilation,
In the awareness that you are supported by all the faithful women of the world, on this truly splendid occasion!

Please know also my precious *Sakinah* that you promote the healing of the entire planet as you receive and give love to your man.
And in this joyous, humble service, you will do wonders to restore the exquisite value of *Al-Islam.*

And as you strive to restore peace to our Earth in the humble service that you do from your home,
The Mercy of The One G-d is with you *Sakinah,* and you will never be left alone!

Now, my dear *Sakinah,* I sincerely pray that you will benefit from this wedding gift that I have left.
For it is offered to you in humility and love, with every hope for your eternal success.

www.ingramcontent.com/pod-product-compliance
Lightning Source LLC
Chambersburg PA
CBHW021334090426
42742CB00008B/599